Morning Notes

Also by Hugh Prather

Shining Through
How to Live in the World and Still Be Happy
The Little Book of Letting Go
Standing on My Head
Notes to Myself
Spiritual Notes to Myself:
    Essential Wisdom for the 21st Century
I Will Never Leave You:
    How Couples Can Achieve the Power of Lasting Love

Morning Notes

365 Meditations to Wake You Up

HUGH PRATHER

Conari Press

First published in 2005 by Conari Press,
an imprint of Red Wheel/Weiser, LLC
York Beach, ME

With offices at:
368 Congress Street
Boston, MA 02210
www.redwheelweiser.com

Library of Congress Cataloging-in-Publication Data

Prather, Hugh.
  Morning notes : 365 meditations to wake you up / Hugh Prather.
    p. cm.
  Includes bibliographical references and index.
  ISBN 1-57324-254-3
  1. Self-realization—Religious aspects—Meditations.
  2. Devotional calendars. I. Title.

BL624.2.P73 2005
158.1'28—dc22

2005014845

Typeset in Janson Text and Triplex Light by Marquardt Art/Design.
Printed in the United States
VG

12 11 10 09 08 07 06 05
 8 7 6 5 4 3 2 1

The paper used in this publication meets the minimum requirements of the
American National Standard for Information Sciences—Permanence of Paper for
Printed Library Materials z39.48-1992 (R1997).

To Beverly Hutchinson
(for so many reasons)

What I Need to Hear

You'll probably notice right off that most of this book is written in the first person. Here's why.

Over the years I have resisted several requests for a book of 365 thoughts because I felt there were a number of excellent ones on the market, and I didn't think I had much to add. But a year or so ago I noticed that I have certain ideas that I keep returning to when I wake up in the morning. The thoughts I need have stabilized and are now like a comfortable old coat with big pockets and extra long sleeves that never fails to keep me warm in winter.

So this book is a little different in that it contains what I personally need to hear—over and over. That's why you'll find the occasional odd entry such as "Today I will do two things: shut up and mind my own business" and "When I'm happy, I don't need to look over my shoulder." Both of these ideas, as well as all the other main thoughts, or "morning notes" for each day, are generalized and expanded upon in the paragraphs that follow them.

My wife Gayle and I have always felt that it cuts

down on mistakes if we begin the day with a clear spiritual goal. We have stacks of sheets listing these daily purposes from the years when we took turns coming up with one. This trading back and forth, and especially our sharing a common objective, was extremely helpful, and we still do something along those same lines. The main change in our spiritual path during the almost forty years we have been married is that we have distilled a multitude of concepts down to just a few, each one simple enough that it can't be fudged. These themes appear throughout this book and constitute a progression of steps.

As I say at one point, "The way out of chaos is to stop analyzing and start experiencing, to stop looking for better ways to say it and start practicing more peaceful and inclusive ways of doing it." If you think about it, all anyone really needs is the golden rule, and if that were practiced daily, it alone would get you where you want to go. Yet most of us find it helpful to have different ways of coming at the subject, and I try to provide a nice variety of concepts along the lines of "treat others as you want to be treated."

I laid out the book so that it can either be used

sequentially or opened at random. Each page is complete in itself.

To me, the most important thing to remember as we set our daily purpose is that there is One who is always with us. We do best when we don't try to go it alone. Instead, we take God's hand, and above all we take God's advice, which can be heard by anyone who just stops a moment and is still. Whether or not this book helps you in your journey, you will arrive Home. We all will. We can make it difficult by insisting that we figure out everything for ourselves or we can make it easy by accepting Help. Easy is best.

To choose love is to begin again.

Clearly, our human family is in distress. Yet because of this, it is also more open to change. Today I join with countless others in a renewed determination to be a better person—a truer parent to children, a more tolerant friend to others, a kinder coworker, a more committed partner. For this to happen, I must make up my mind, because behavior that flows from conflicted thoughts can't be controlled. Engaging in trench warfare with my personality doesn't work. Nor does making resolutions that last only days or weeks. To succeed I must unite my mind around a single purpose. And love is the only true purpose, and the only real unity.

2

I know what to do.
The only *question* is, will I do it.

I have never lived this day before. I am free to start fresh. My mistakes are in the past. They can be my shame or my treasure of useful indicators. I will use them to renew my faith and strengthen my resolve. Because of my mistakes, I know what to do. Today I release the old ways that have split my mind and drained my power. I will fill my thoughts with the newness of love and the simplicity of peace. Today I open myself to others so that I may open my heart to God.

3

The answer is to let go of pressure, not add more.

My tendency is to make matters worse. Let me at least pause a moment and see what I want to do. When I set up a war within my mind, I put it between myself and God, because I make conflict more important than everything else. When I try to thwart other people, winning becomes more valuable to me than Love. And when I try to dictate the course of events, I am immediately at odds with the situation I'm already in. Yet when I relax into equality and trust in a greater Reality, life becomes simpler and my behavior modifies itself naturally.

4

To free myself from useless battles,
I put all things in God's hands.

Sooner or later, I must take a leap of faith. The
existence of a sustaining Love makes no rational
sense. It can only be felt when I exercise trust.
As long as I wait for signs, miracles, fulfillment
of dreams, or just a slight improvement in
circumstances, I will never know Reality. The
divine can only be seen through the eyes of faith.
Today I will proceed as if I already believe.

5

Because the truth is true, letting go is all there is to do.

Everything I do today is like a little test. Do I want the question or the answer, mental conflict or peace, to be right or happy, to be a burden to others or a blessing, to awake or continue sleeping? Each decision I make moves me a step closer to Home or a step further away. Therefore, it's clear that since the choice is between Truth and error, all I need do is to question—and thereby release—my desire to continue making the same mistakes.

6

Instead of trying to force the day I want, let me embrace the day I am given.

Change begins with the willingness to make a modest effort each day. To at least try to let God be God, to let Truth be my truth. I betray what I believe when I push against events and other people. Naturally, if some change is helpful to me or another, I make it. But it's simply a fact that life is happier when I listen to the music behind the scenery than when I nosily try to rearrange it.

7

To be in God is simply to be connected.

I need something more than free will, independence, or specialness. I need something more than private thoughts, a personal code, or a splendid point of view. I need people. Not in order to stay alive but in order to be fully alive, fully human, to be affectionate, funny, playful, generous, happy. I can love a concept—I can study it, meditate on it, and repeat it to others—but I can't throw my arms around it. And that's what God is: arms around us all.

8

Oneness is not cooperation.
It is experiencing
the familiar in another.

No one owes me anything. No one is obliged to
meet my needs. People are people. They are not
sexual experiences or career support or a series of
well-wishers on my daily rounds. They are not
enemies of my enemies or my personal support
group or a way of killing time. People are not even
a means for us to "get to the next level." They don't
exist to give to us, or to withhold. They *are* us.

9

The only cost of forgiveness is to again be whole.

Isn't it obvious that anyone who wants to forgive forgives easily? I must not underestimate my desire to continue judging. But the problem with grievances, grudges, bitterness, and hurt feelings is that I have to remain damaged. I have to remain living proof of the other person's guilt.

10

When I see your heart, I want what you want.

"Love your neighbor as yourself" implies nothing more complicated than the fact that anything less than love is not love. The golden rule is not asking "What would *I* want?" The question is what does my child, my friend, my partner, my parent truly want? Love does not guess; it enfolds, embraces, and understands. If we do not love someone outside ourselves, then quite simply, we do not love ourselves. God is love, and within the love of God there is no discrimination.

Kindness is the touch of God.

If God is love, kindness is the key to happiness, freedom, and true success. And if God is one, it is impossible that the practice of love would mean choosing between myself and another. I am being dishonest when I say that I must put myself first. I must put love first. Today I will use the most powerful and transformative of all spiritual practices: I will be kind. I will be kind to myself, to everyone I encounter, and to everyone who crosses my mind.

12

All around us is a welcoming Presence, but only by being kind can I feel it.

A gentle affect can disguise a malicious intent. Kindness is not smiling or agreeing or speaking softly. It must come from my heart and if expressed, always include a silent blessing. Letting people know that I hold them in my prayers sometimes engages my ego because of the acknowledgment I seek. At other times, telling them that I am praying for them can be a way of connecting and showing support. Kindness must dictate the form my efforts take. Every living thing is held in endless blessing by the divine. By being like God, we feel God.

13

When I submit to Truth, I submit to harmlessness.

Submitting is not saying yes to every ego request or condoning destructive behavior in myself or others. It has nothing to do with indecisive stands, shaky loyalties, or "seeing both sides" when a friend has been mistreated. Submitting is an impulse of sincerity, not an act of passivity or a show of impartiality. It is focusing sharply on my deeper self rather than on the superficial. My behavior is filled with God only when my heart is filled with God.

14

By letting go, I fall into God.

If I "let go and let God," I *allow* Love to be within me. I quietly acknowledge and embrace my true nature. Letting Love is extending love, looking gently, being quick to understand and slow to judge. It is relaxing, being still, accepting, and above all, giving up the illusion of control.

15

The ego is always up to something.
Unless I remain conscious,
I will act it out in some way.

An action can't exclude the mind of the one who
acts. My behavior may seem appealing or unappeal-
ing, admirable or objectionable, depending on the
reactions of those who view it. But another's take
on what I do doesn't alter my intent, which is the
true content of my behavior. Since all minds are
connected, the deeper effect of my actions is in what
I think. That is why there are no private thoughts
or completely hidden motives. I can't expect to be
a person who consistently makes life easier on my
loved ones if I don't stay aware of my thoughts.

16

We can accept one another
and enjoy life, or judge
one another and be unhappy.

Self-preoccupation is an unhappy state of mind, yet it offers several temporary pleasures, and these must be honestly looked at. For example, revenge can seem deeply satisfying for a while and acts of ill will can make us feel more confident. But there is another set of pleasures that comes from empathy, tolerance, and trusting other people's processes, which never leads to misery. If there is indeed a greater Guidance, who am I to know what anyone else should be doing? *This* is what is meant by trusting others.

17

Closeness to God is first experienced as closeness to others.

There are personality types that are universally disliked. There are also individuals who are destructive, even murderous. Yet personality is not all there is to anyone. The experience of connection isn't dependent on how others talk to me or behave. Nor is it a matter of making someone like me. If we can feel close to individuals who are miles away or even to people after they die, surely the potential exists to be at peace with those who are physically present.

18

A gentle and accepting mind always feels close to God.

I alone block my perception of Oneness by thinking defensively. It may be rational to fear someone physically, but not spiritually. God does not hold me back from feeling close to anyone—telemarketer, teenager, politician, postal worker, cable company executive, spouse, or self-help author. When I relax my mind, my vision can now move past the surface of things, and there, awaiting me, is a great Splendor.

19

Make your state of mind more important than what you are doing.

Only the mind can be controlled. Health, income, relationships, longevity, reputation, and the like, can't be controlled. Personal destiny is merely the story told by my body. Even the tiniest event can't be controlled, and the attempt to do so always splits the mind. In trying to control what I believe to be outside my mind, I discount the power of my thoughts and fail to take responsibility for them.

20

Inner peace is letting go of being right.

Obviously, I can't make myself right without making someone else wrong. Forgiveness is a choice. If I want to change my mind from an environment that tortures me to an environment that comforts me, I must make forgiving as routine as breathing. Forgiveness isn't something nice I do for another person; it's something nice I do for my mental health.

21

Acceptance is the way
I bless myself.

My disdain, dismissal, hatred, or dislike of another does not punish that individual. It punishes me. I am the one with the bitter mind. I can't pass on that little piece of hell to another. Hatred destroys all awareness of light within me, but unless I go out of my way to make others aware of it, they don't even know I judge them.

22

Our core is already positive. Choice is made possible by seeing how we routinely betray our core.

If I look at a shadow closely enough, I see that it's merely a shadow. I release my negative impulses and thoughts by giving them more attention, not less. No one acts out a judgment of which they are acutely aware. No one makes a conscious decision to act insanely against their own interests.

23

If we are each in God's hands,
judging another
is an act of arrogance.

I merely delude myself if I think it is possible to
judge. How could I know a faster or better way to
transform another person's heart than the way God
has already chosen? Judging is a not so subtle way
of procrastinating, of putting off something I need
to take responsibility for this instant. What am I
avoiding that I am taking time to judge?

24

How could one person's way possibly be superior to another person's way if God is leading us all?

If I believe that my spiritual path is superior, my path is not spiritual. Spirit is One. The divine doesn't contain degrees of correctness. Either we all share the same Truth and ultimate destiny, or there is no truth and we are lost in a reality of private perception and momentary interpretation. The way out of chaos is to stop analyzing and start experiencing, to stop looking for better ways to say it and start practicing more peaceful and inclusive ways of doing it.

25

All thoughts are equally a part of the mind.

Notice how difficult it is merely to think in peace about *any* individual who comes to mind. Still, that must be my aim if I am ever to experience consistent mental wholeness. My tendency is to disown the negative parts of my mind because it's uncomfortable to admit what they say about me. Yet I think what I think by choice. All of it is my mind. My motivation to learn how to react peacefully to those who people my thoughts should be enormous—once I consider the effects my attitudes have on me.

26

I release you from your past,
that I may see you
as God sees you.

In conversations, those who are not present are
often described in terms of their mistakes. Even
individuals before us now are seen as stories and
not as they are this instant. In faithlessness we think,
"You are created in the image and likeness of your
past." Yet it's not mentally dishonest to focus instead
on what is fresh, different, and unexpected. The
encounter I am having now has never occurred
before. Except on a spiritual level, no one is ever
the same, and their progress will not be evident if
I only stare at the decisions I have already made
about them.

27

We each journey on a path of mistakes.

When I look back, I don't have a consistent interpretation of which acts were victories or defeats. And I have seen the same childhood circumstances as both damaging and beneficial. This much is clear: Many important gains have come on the heels of my greatest mistakes. Progress is the process of correcting mistakes, not of being perfect. Today I will make starting over more important than looking back. Those who make no mistakes have already arrived. I simply don't know what mistakes anyone needs to make. Therefore, I am in no position to be "helpful."

28

True helpfulness comes from connection, not from words.

Words alone don't help. It is what God speaks in our hearts when we read or hear words that helps. That's why familiar passages from sacred scripture often mean something new each time we reread them. And that's why it never works for me to decide what someone else needs to hear. If I want to be of use today, I must focus on my feeling of connection with others, because God is heard within the experience of love.

29

Trusting a greater Reality makes relationships easier.

When I judge others, I question the innocence God has placed within them. Seeing my mistake, I must immediately put them back in God's hands. Today I will acknowledge that I really don't know how hard people try, how far they may have come, or in what ways God is transforming them this very instant. Comparing is the opposite of relating. Going Home is not a foot race in which I compete. To conclude that I am ahead or behind another, I must first break with the peace of Oneness.

30

Only love can discern the bridge
that stretches between two hearts.
In love it is seen,
and in love it is crossed.

What another person does has no fixed meaning.
I interpret behavior as I choose. What do I want
it to mean? I perceive others through either my
moods or my peace. Stillness sees oneness; moods
see chaos. Don't fight thoughts; change the source.
Since I am responsible for which part of my mind
I use, today I will keep returning to my quiet mind.

31

Dare to be ordinary.

God is One. I experience God by experiencing equality: the sameness in another person and the divinity in all living things. Today I will dare to turn my back on the world's shrill urgings that we should each strive to be the best. Instead, I will embrace my ordinariness. I will be normal and equal. I will have no "spiritual" posture, tell no ego-enhancing "spiritual" stories, think no separating "spiritual" thoughts. I did not create myself, and today I will relax into who I already am.

32

God knows the way to my heart.

God is not nearer just because we think about God. God could not be nearer. God's strength is our strength. God's life is our life. God's happiness is our happiness. We are each made out of God. Even now, God breathes into us our purpose, our motivation, and our fulfillment.

33

Discouragement is not helpful.

Discouragement is love of the ego because it turns to the ego for its sense of reality. Spirit will not and cannot confirm "low spirits." Discouragement is never necessary. And it isn't much fun. But the answer is not to fight it. If I fight it, I make myself a victim of my own mind, which is impossible. When I am discouraged, no matter how slight the feeling, I will be still a moment and find the place in me where I am whole. I will let my mind fall gently back into place. Then, I will start over by doing just one thing without discouragement.

34

Whatever I worry about is not worth worrying about.

Stillness, not worry, plumbs the depth of my potential. If I want to have a deep sense of freedom, be attuned to my intuition, and remember the beauty in those around me, worry is of no use. Today I will confront my ego directly whenever I worry. I will ask, "Just what is it you suggest I do?" In this way I see that the aim of the worried part of my mind is not to improve the future. In fact, it has nothing to do with the future. The aim of worry is always to disrupt the present by undercutting connection and peace, which can only be experienced now.

35

There are no questions in God.

Today is the day I stop arguing with myself about whether the divine is logical or Truth is true. Questioning whether it is reasonable to be kind, to believe in a higher Reality, or to act from faith is merely my desire to put off practicing today. Yet only practice brings understanding. It's arrogant to think that somehow I *need* my "intellectual honesty," my wise and profound questions. What does doubt have to do with Love? My aim today will be to let all questions dissolve within the stillness of my heart and the gentleness of my actions.

36

Adding light to darkness solves the problem of darkness.

My thoughts constitute the happiness or misery in which I live. When I battle my thoughts, I split my mind and put myself in a firefight with shifting realities. However, I can safely leave all conflicted thoughts in place if I merely add God to them. No matter how strident my ego, it can't completely drown out God's quiet reassurance. Today, all I need do is worry in peace, be discouraged in peace, be confused in peace, and so on. There is always music behind the discord, if I choose to hear it.

37

Fear is my responsibility because fear means that I am conflicted.

We are like children pointing and screaming at a shadow, and all the while a loving parent stands beside us offering comfort and safety. God shows us the place where we are invulnerable and completely at peace. Yet if I am conflicted about moving in that direction, the peace of God doesn't force me to decide against my desires, even though those inclinations, no matter how tentatively or erratically followed, always hurt me. Today, when I notice I am afraid, I will examine my mind for conflicting purposes.

38

The means I use to change my mental state becomes my new state of mind.

I can't force my mind to be whole, because force itself is mental. Pressure in any form is war. When part of my mind tries to force another part to change, the outcome is mental upset. However, if I focus my full attention on wholeness, my mind becomes whole. When stillness and peace are the means, stillness and peace are the result.

39

Just one thought of blessing recreates me in its image.

I intend to pray for others, but so often I forget or do it halfheartedly. Perhaps this is because sincere gifts from a loving mind are given without calculation, and prayer by its very nature is anonymous. But it is not without effects on the one who prays. As I go through the day, I will try to notice any damaged images I carry about anyone I see or think of, and I will correct them on the spot.

40

Awareness disarms my ego.

Our busy, conflicted mind never forgives, for only peace can see innocence. Whenever I fall back into my ego, all the old stuff is still there. There is no way to perfect it, but there is a way to disarm it. When I look long and carefully at my judgments, when I "look the beast in the eye," I begin to see that these are not my deepest feelings. But I must stay with that process long enough that I truly do perceive a different side of me and not just sugarcoat the mental contents with pleasant words.

41

My mind is a gift.
Its nature is pure.

There is no tension in simply being what I am.
Letting go and relaxing are the same. I have to
work quite hard to be unlike the child God created.
Tension is a clue that I am at odds with my function
and my destiny. Therefore I will settle into the day
as it unfolds. There is nothing to figure out and no
sales pitch I need give myself about who I am.
There is One who knows what I am all about and
never forgets. I am relieved of that task.

42

See your ego's plan for you clearly and you can't help but laugh.

Forgiveness is not a state of mind in which no judgmental thoughts about myself or others occur, but one in which they show themselves to be utter nonsense. I know when I have reached that point when, even though I am conscious of the thoughts, they no longer make me anxious or stir me up. In fact, if my forgiveness work has been thorough, the unforgiving thoughts are seen as laughably absurd.

43

Wallowing in guilt
is self-indulgent.

To indulge in thoughts of guilt, remorse, and regret seems virtuous, an act of humility or honesty. But it's actually a failure to take responsibility for my past actions, because it's still all about *me*. These thoughts don't help or heal the individuals I have hurt. I must interrupt my self-attack and give the blessings I have withheld. Often this is best done silently, since the consequences of making amends directly are unpredictable. The decision to bless comes from within and includes the intuition of whether or not to act.

44

Attack is the problem, not the answer.

I am making the same mistake in a different form when I indulge in shame, guilt, or self-loathing— first I hurt this person; now I am hurting myself. Justification for attack does not hinge on the object of the attack. Attack in any form blocks the experience of peace.

45

I cannot betray myself by "loving too much."

What could I possibly lose by seeking the peace of another person—literally making another's peace my single-minded goal? I can certainly lose by destroying another's peace; in fact, loss will be the one reliable outcome. And I can lose by loving too little and thereby making myself small. But to "love too much" is merely to be my self, to be my own heart, to be my true and deepest nature, which is all I have ever wanted to be. Real love isn't "balanced" and can't be measured or quantified.

46

Love is a preview of heaven.

Love is not just our way out of fear, it is our destination point and our fulfillment. In the words of the apostle John: *Love one another, because love is of God. And everyone who loves is born of God and knows God. But the unloving know nothing of God, for God is love.*

47

The jailer is also in jail.

Freedom is found in little things—in errands and tasks and small encounters. Today I will practice freedom by remaining aware of the situation I am in, the individuals who are present, and the quality of my thoughts. I will not force my thoughts, but simply stay conscious of the sentence layer of my mind, which tends to focus narrowly on who or what needs to change. In wanting to control, I am automatically controlled. Instead I will *extend* freedom by putting no pressure on other people and making no attempt to micromanage events. I will do what I do with flexibility and ease and a steady, peaceful awareness.

48

If I don't need anything from you, I am free to think of you in peace.

The moment I want something from another person, my happiness is compromised. Each time I try to influence someone, I set myself up as a victim, because it's impossible to get perfect cooperation from anyone. Today I will observe that I survive just fine without my expectations being met or my demands obeyed. In fact, in letting go, I am left with the peace that is already mine.

49

Every hour I am focused
on the future, I suffer
an hour's loss of this life.

Clearly, to dwell on the future or the past is to avoid living now. The present can be scary because so often it's associated with emotional or physical pain. Pain may be a means of bringing one back to the present, but it is not the only means. Stillness is also centered in now, but a now of an entirely different sort. The quiet now is very broad and reliable. It contains no dread, no jolting interruptions, and no abrupt beginnings. Beauty shines from every aspect, and peace is the gift both given and received.

50

The longest strides
come from standing still.

The paradox of progress is that we grow each time we realize that we can only be where we are. I can't fail to grow in happiness, wholeness, generosity, and inner strength when I am quieter mentally, more peaceful, and above all, more present.

51

I will give peace
with my thoughts and cause
no harm with my words.

We enter the awareness of many people in the
course of a day. With each encounter there is a little
exchange, and we leave something behind. This
trail, and not our individual accomplishments, is
our legacy to the world. At the end of my life, what
tracks do I want to look back and see?

52

If God holds me, why am I holding on?

As I grow older, I am able to do increasingly less, yet my mind doesn't seem to age. Yes, brain functions like memory and calculating skills have deteriorated some, but the "I" that I am remains the same. It seems clear that my real safety lies in the recognition that whether I am physically paralyzed, compulsively hyperactive, or somewhere in between, I still remain as God created me. Therefore I can safely say, "Today I hold onto nothing, because God holds on to me."

53

My mind is like a hand
that can open or clench.
The choice is mine.

If I am capable of tightening my mental grip, I am
also capable of loosening it. I am free to let go of
wanting and getting, having and losing, worrying
and denying, all of which require me to narrow
my mind. A relaxed mind can't sustain a fearful or
judgmental focus. Today I will notice each time my
mind tightens, for if the divine is real, I can rest in
the truth that there is nowhere else I need be and
nothing else I must have.

54

God's light shines
in all directions.

To heal the past, just dance backward through the
rays of God, which shine through every step you
ever took. They were always there, even though you
chose to close your eyes. Then dance back to your
home within the present. But leave the door open
wide behind you to such brilliant shadows and
healing memories.

55

Wherever I go,
God is already there.

From your heart, the River of God flows gently into the future. Immerse every fearful expectation within the still and silent waters of divine blessing. Then watch as the River washes each anticipation, now sparkling with welcome, onto the shore of your tomorrow.

56

Repeatedly assessing
past performance is failure
to concentrate on what
can be done now.

Today, each time I feel even a slight stab of defeat
or disappointment, I will be still and remember
that God is not mistaken in loving me. I will sense
this love deep within me, and I will watch as it
quietly replaces all shame and anguish with a fresh
determination to do the best I can this moment.

57

"Trust yourself" and "Trust God"
are not conflicting ideals.
I must trust what I am,
but what I am is never alone.

It's impossible to choose without conflict between
being selfless or selfish. The first choice makes me
feel self-neglectful and the second, self-indulgent. To
"sacrifice" for others makes me resentful and can lead
to hatred, yet to disregard their needs, isolates me
and may lead to a deep loneliness. But the choice
between the two is always false because God is both
love and peace. God's love blesses each and all equally,
and to choose God is to choose peace. When I ask
myself, "What is the most peaceful thing to do?"
the answer is what I *want* to do, and it is kind to all.

58

Today I will see through the eyes of Love.

I am called to a great wedding. I am asked to embrace Life everywhere I look. Life's vision sees the threads of innocence woven through all people and things, like a shaft of light falling across treasured objects long hidden in darkness. Because I am real, and because Life is real, I must already be a part of Life, and it a part of me. There is a place in me so harmless and still that all fear has dropped away. As snow unifies a landscape and moonlight transforms it, today my vision will arise from this place, and it will blanket the world in peace.

59

When I extend what I am, I broaden my happiness.

Nice people are always happier than mean people. To expand and extend the love in my heart creates in me an innocent vision. It doesn't reform other egos, but it does see beyond them. This seeing is not mere illumination, like shining a flashlight on a trash heap. Spiritual sight is spiritual reality. What is seen in love is at one with the seeing. Nothing has more substance and presence than accurate perception. Ego perception is arbitrary and unstable, but to look gently is to begin to see heaven at hand.

60

Blessed are those who try again.

Trying again is an act of faith, not in predictable outcomes, but in predictable blessings. We reach a time in life when we see that things have not turned out as we believed in our youth they would. We become afraid to hope, afraid to try again. We especially tend to be cynical about forming new friendships or finding a potential partner. Then the possibility of a new relationship opens up, or the potential of an old one is recognized, for never does God stop presenting opportunities. Naturally, a part of us is skeptical and holds back. We think that protecting ourselves is more important than loving another person. But nothing is more important than love.

61

"I am completely at peace
with the way you are."

I tell myself that the people I know are in God's
hands, but do I believe it? For if God loves us all
equally and guides us all impartially, why do I keep
expecting people to behave differently? Today,
whenever some behavior does not meet with my
approval, I will silently say, "Because God is real,
it is possible for me to be at peace with what you
just did."

62

The one I hold myself superior to is a part of me.

Obviously some things, whether certain people, dogs, weather conditions, or insects, are more destructive than others. Yet on the level of their core, one individual is *not* less spiritual than another. It's impossible to be enlightened and know it. Enlightenment is awareness of oneness, of which there is no consistent symbol in the world. The monsters of history all lacked awareness of oneness, and my own worst moments have been when I have lost sight of it. My goal today is to be vigilant for feelings of superiority and to correct all thoughts that any personal attribute could set me apart from what is real and lasting in others.

63

Today I will do two things:
shut up and
mind my own business.

Ninety percent of my relationship problems would
be solved virtually overnight if I would just learn to
shut up. I simply don't know when someone needs
to hear what I have to say. But when I think I do
know, I clearly am not hearing the part of me that
I should be listening to.

64

Is it likely that what God wants will be thwarted?

The Shepherd returns all lambs to the fold; the Father welcomes home even the prodigal son who has "sinned against heaven." I will not be arrogant and think I am the one problem beyond God's capacity, that I am the one person who can thwart God's will. As I go through the day, I will be "humble in the Lord."

65

Today I will remember God.

We have been told that God is love. We have been told that God is always with us. We have been told that even if we make our bed in hell, God is there. We have been told that God's peace has been given to us and left in our keeping. We have even been told that it is God's great pleasure to give us the Kingdom. There may be room for overconfidence, but there is certainly no room for confusion.

66

Faith is the willingness
to rest in the arms
that already hold me.

The bully is usually the leader of the playground,
the ruthless often climb the corporate ladder faster,
politicians willing to lie routinely get reelected, and
mean people frequently live longer than nice people.
Goodness is seldom rewarded in the world. But
goodness *is* rewarded. And the reward is immediate,
because only those committed to being good
experience peace, which transcends the world.

67

Faith can be redirected.

A true and helpful faith is not reliance on something
I would expect to happen judging from my past
experience. The events of my life don't exactly
inspire faith! Yet I always see what I choose to see.
I have a sustainable faith only when I extend it.
This I do by acknowledging precisely what can be
relied on in others. True faith carries with it a state
of joining, a state of comfort, a state of Family—
provided that I don't search my life for individual
"blessings." I am not special, and this recognition,
honestly seen, is the foundation of a new kind
of faith.

68

Faith is a willingness to rest within the present.

Faith is not an argument or a demonstration. It requires no subsequent results or logical validation. Nor is it the result of signs and wonders. It is experienced instantly when welcomed, and it leaves only comfort within. Once faith has delivered us to the peace of God, it is no longer needed.

69

The way Home
is greater than me.

Today I will take note of every personal conclusion
I trip over and of each predisposition I stumble into.
I can walk unwaveringly on the path of Oneness,
or I can be right. But note that what I think is right
one moment is soon discarded for a different
opinion, causing still another change in direction.
To proceed steadfastly, I must think humbly by
acknowledging a Wisdom greater than my own.

70

My precious opinions never made anyone happy— including me.

Wholeness is an overall condition of the mind itself and is not found in a rigid set of beliefs. The sentence layer of the mind is incapable of wholeness because words are mere symbols, and they differ for each individual. When friends, couples, or family members focus on words rather than the intent of each other's heart, the individuals feel more separate. Yet when the heart desires of each person are taken into consideration, an increased sense of closeness and happiness results.

71

Happiness is peace, not comparison.

There is no greater fear than the fear of being happy, because happiness threatens our ego autonomy. To be happy we would have to give up our unhappy opinions of other people. If the people in our lives were profoundly innocent, we think this would reflect badly on us—because we believe that a comparison is all we are. Today I will remember that within Love there are no rankings, no distinctions, and no hierarchy.

72

God holds me in light.

Today I will be starlight and crisp bracing air and a deep blue darkness. I will be spring rain and fresh fields of grass. I will be shouts of laughter from parks and pools and soft sand beaches. I will be purring and petting and barks at high-tossed balls. I will be peace within the heart, silence within the mind, and love blazing from the eyes. I will be that which touches things equally and leaves no soul untouched. And I will laugh gently at the notion that I must contrast myself with anyone.

73

God is peace.

When you feel carried along and experience no hesitation in what you do. When you feel no necessity to interpret each distinction and every detail. When you can think of those around you comfortably. And when time and your body are no longer a preoccupation. Then you have no need to ask God for special information and personalized guidance. Therefore, I make my goal to move through the day in simple peace, for God *is* peace.

74

The choice is always between my quiet mind and my busy mind.

Whenever possible, I will turn my moments of asking into moments of silent listening and gentle watching. My function today is to step quietly around disbelief and confusion. I will stop heeding and reacting to my agitated ego and make instead a peaceful flow of thoughts my goal and my preoccupation.

75

The answer to prayer
is not withheld until later.

A future would be necessary only if it provided
me with what I presently lack. But what could be
lacking in God? Our spiritual path is a shift from
a dream of needs to a consciousness of wholeness.
Today I will choose my desires for the present over
my desires for the future by asking, "How can I feel
my connection to God this instant?"

76

Resistance to stillness is attraction to conflict.

Things fall into place more easily when I am not conflicted about what I'm doing. However, my tendency is to act without dealing with the conflict. Trying to overpower conflict by just barging ahead with the next activity or by merely saying positive things to myself, doesn't work—because it's dishonest. Since conflict is not a part of Truth, it can be fully acknowledged, then gently bypassed. All that's needed is for me to pause a moment and see what I want to do. The resistance I feel to taking this step is my desire to be unconscious and confused, in other words, to be a victim.

77

My perceptions reflect their source.

Because the divine is all around us, we can turn our perceptions over to God and partake of healing imagery and peaceful considerations, even though the picture before us may initially be quite bleak. There is no limit to the number of thoughts we can think that reflect Love, nor can the world remain unaffected by a gentle mental outpouring.

78

God made me whole
and God is everlasting.

What do I need from another ego that God has not already given me? Is there a gap in eternity? Are there parentheses in Truth? If I am incomplete, my Source could not be whole. To be one with another, even for an instant, is to have everything, for God is One.

79

Being tolerant is healthier
than being
separate or controlling.

True healing includes the recognition that we never
suffer alone. Thus healing ourselves is an act of
generosity, not of self-indulgence. Each degree of
spiritual progress is fueled by an increased awareness of our effect on others. Today I will remain
aware of connection, for therein lies true health.

80

Treat your body as you would treat your beloved pet.

Most of us have a more balanced sense of how to identify with a dog than with our body. We love our dog today, but we can't love our body because we are waiting for it to be different. Free of the anger that comes from unreasonable expectations, we feed our dog a good, simple diet. We exercise him and bathe him and take him to get his shots. We keep him away from dangerous situations and gently decline to give him everything he thinks he wants. There is no war in this relationship because there is neither neglect nor a battle for perfection. A sane approach to questions about diet, exercise, sleep, and the like is to ask, "If my body were my beloved pet, what would I do?"

81

Without forgiveness, I live in a hostile world.

The problem is not "needing to forgive" one's father, mother, partner, ex-spouse, third grade teacher, or supervisor at work. The problem is unforgiveness itself. Until I question the need to judge altogether and stop reserving the right to be right, I remain alone in the world. No living thing is wholly welcome in my mind, and no individual has a reliable place in my heart.

82

Your comfort is my own.

Today my silent pledge to my loved ones is this:
I want you to feel free of self-consciousness when
you are around me—even if you are upset. I want
you to be able to say anything to me—even what
you don't mean. I want you to be so comfortable
that you don't even think it's necessary to notice I'm
here. The experience of Love includes no need for
me to be defensive. Nor does it demand that I be
respected, honored, or acknowledged.

83

I alone block my ability to see Beauty.

Preoccupation with another person's ego blocks my vision. To see the heart of another, first I must be honest with myself about exactly what it is I am making more important than love. Second, I must allow that individual to be the way they are at this moment. Now my vision can show me something new and totally free of my opinions. No issue should ever be made more important than the relationship.

84

There is no love without acceptance.

Clearly, loved ones should try to accommodate each other—they should in fact rush to meet each other's needs—but accommodation doesn't improve a relationship if it's forced. All I can do is try to do my part, knowing that for me to apply pressure, make demands, or "set boundaries" in order to force loved ones to do their part, always makes a bad situation worse. Real love between partners, friends, parent and child, or between any two is sustained by a deep familiarity with each other's weaknesses and needs, and it includes a profound willingness to receive in our heart the way the other person wishes to feel and act.

85

Today I will discard a few problems from the list of the ones I think I need.

So that I may have a chance of being happy today, I will practice being whole, feeling whole, and living from wholeness. Problems shatter wholeness and so I will question whether I need all the ones I have kept. Furthermore, I will fail to obsess on the problem du jour.

86

Awareness of God doesn't give me a charmed life. It gives me awareness of God.

There is no reward in the world for our spiritual progress. The Eternal doesn't comp us with more and more things that always change. Spirit doesn't give me the unspiritual, and God doesn't "bless" me with money for thinking the right thoughts. In fact, trying to use my mind to acquire is always anxiety provoking. It should be obvious that only everlasting gifts can come from the Everlasting. So I can stop looking around for my spiritual perks. That alone should eliminate a major distraction to spiritual focus.

87

If I am a part of God,
I must do my part.

The part of us that touches God, we must touch.
The part of us that hears heaven's song, we must
hear. The part of us that feels the comfort of Home,
we must feel. Be still, and it is accomplished.

88

Let my first response be stillness.

Because stillness resides in my heart, not in circumstances, it need never be delayed until a more convenient time. Because stillness is the presence of peace, not the absence of noise, it is always present.

89

True solitude includes connection.

It makes no sense to say that in order to feel that which joins us all, we must get away from each other. To know stillness, I need not rearrange my life, merely my values. To know stillness, I need only give it respect.

90

I can't have the life I want,
but I can be at peace
with the life I have.

A daily practice of prayer and meditation has a cumulative effect, but the effect is within the heart. Spiritual practices do not eliminate accidents, mistakes, tragedies, and suffering. But a deep turning to God unites the mind and brings it peace. It lifts the spirit and begins to set it free, and it can imbue ordinary events with beauty and enjoyment. Prayer and meditation won't get me a new life, but if I'm sincere, I just may fall in love with the life I already have.

91

Love is the mind of God— and it is my mind also.

The ego has no home and no companion. It lives in anxiety and misunderstanding. It can't enjoy because it can't stay in the present. It can't love because it can't see without criticizing. Surely I want to be more than an ego, to experience a deep and comfortable bond with others, to look with peace instead of righteousness, to be happy instead of justified.

92

If there's a question whether to say it, don't say it.

Love is a state of grace, a way of seeing and blessing, yet its test is not that it seems pleasant and nice. It must be genuine. I always know if my intention comes from my heart, because I feel no hesitation, no small sense of conflict before I speak. I should always support and advocate for any loved one who needs and wants my help and any child I am in a position to assist, and my stand may at times appear unyielding. But *I* know what it truly is. Yet if I am conflicted as I start to speak, my ego is already involved and it's better to wait until I feel clear, because conflict will accompany whatever conflict motivates.

93

The heart can listen better than the ears.

People converse on two levels: subject matter and feelings. Rarely are the words of an exchange what the conversation is actually about, yet we usually overinterpret and overreact to what the other person says, and even loving relationships sometimes break up over mundane discussions. In the exchanges I have today, I will silently ask, "What does (*name of person*) really want from me?" More often than not, people want merely to be respected and supported. They want to be understood and appreciated. It's really not complicated, unless I get all caught up in the words they use or the subjects they choose.

94

Empathy is not a behavior; it's an inner necessity.

It isn't necessary to speak to other people or to agree with them or to cheer them up or to spend more time with them. But it is necessary to identify with them, to love them as myself. If I can identify with my pets and plants, I can certainly identify with other human beings. I know what it's like to feel understood.

95

In stillness
I will ask what God sees.

There is a sense in which the world has purpose
and meaning and individuals are perfect just the
way they are. Obviously that's not how it looks, and
telling people in pain that "everything happens for
a reason" is flat out cruel. But when we are still we
can sometimes sense that there is another take on all
this insanity. So today I will let the world be the way
it is, and I will silently ask what God sees in each
person's heart that I don't see.

96

I am at liberty to notice God's presence wherever I look.

If God is in my mind, then God can be seen in what I choose to notice or think about. And if God is a part of all living things, then everywhere I look, God looks back at me.

97

A still mind cannot create chaos.
A conflicted mind can
create nothing else.

How can peace be welcomed into an unpeaceful heart? How can quietness be received by a busy mind? How can I know love if I cherish unloving thoughts? How can I be aware of the eternal and changeless if I am centered on my desire for something to change? To experience God, I must become as still as God.

98

God's gifts
are given in gratitude.

No worldly effort is fairly perceived or fairly treated.
Yet every spiritual effort is treated with perfect
fairness and is known even as the desire to make it
fills our heart. The gifts of God are not only "just
compensation" for our steadfastness; they are
wrapped in stillness, tied in beauty, and handed
to us in everlasting gratitude.

99

Problems do not justify unkindness.

Few things need to be done all at once, and very little needs to be done in a hurry. When trying to solve a problem, I must open myself to all options, including taking small steps and making modest improvements as I go along, instead of doggedly insisting on a one-time solution. No problem is solved perfectly and all problems leave some residue. My chronic need to rush, signals that I am willing to attack my body and fracture my mind. Kindness to myself as well as to others must be a part of the process or else it is ultimately meaningless.

100

Pour time generously over all your tasks.

I notice that when I place myself under a time constraint, when I set a deadline and rush to meet it, it's virtually impossible to keep from outwardly blaming or mentally attacking other people. Yet time can be a lubricant as well as a point of friction. Today I will give myself, my mind, and all that I do more than enough time.

101

God's holy peace is all around me.
When I am still,
it is reflected within me.

One thing for certain I know about myself and
everyone I've met. We are doing too much. We
need to stop setting up hoops to jump through. We
need to stop second-guessing ourselves. We need to
stop tallying up what we fail to accomplish as we go
through the day. We need to be quiet. We need to
be happy. We need to be still.

102

Make the peace of God more important than daily tasks.

It's essential to plot a course, to set a purpose, to have a way. Within the bewildering array of concepts presented by the world, what will be my direction at the start of the day; what will be my path? This question addresses my heart's purpose, not my to-do list of duties and chores. It is infinitely more important than brushing my teeth in circles, winning the war with my hair, eating a "good" breakfast, exercising "long enough," rushing "to get ready," or any other priority I may habitually have upon rising.

103

I will remember the One who holds my hand in love.

There is One who is always with us, and so as we wake in the morning, we never need to start our day alone. We always have the option of beginning by first feeling God's comfort and blessing, which was with us throughout the night and will be with us throughout this day, this life, and forever.

104

Simply stop a moment
and stand in
God's holy light.

What is more important than being real? What could possibly come before experiencing what I am and where I am? If eternity is my Home, why not visit Home now? Today I will pause often to bask in God's love.

 **105**

God's voice
is within me.

We must not be afraid to trust ourselves, to think our own thoughts, to decide what course to take, and to walk gently and easily toward our goal. The One who is with us speaks not from a distance, but from within.

106

Time is always put to some use.

How valuable I believe I am determines how I use
my time. Do I accept myself as God sees me? If my
attitude is that I am of little meaning, I won't assign
a high value to my time, and I'll pay little attention
to how I handle it. Time can be used to draw closer
to Home or to move further away, but there is no
neutral way to use time.

107

No matter how often or how long ago I made the mistake, it's never too late to correct it.

Even a tentative step toward light is better than remaining in darkness. Mistakes, including persistent ones, don't define me unless I just want to believe they do. Although many of my patterns have been long term and perverse, no one can succeed in recreating their spiritual self. Making the same mistake does not justify feeling hopeless. Nothing prevents me from changing course. What small step can be taken now? This day—in fact, even this life—is not lost as long as there is still a moment left to begin again.

108

Because God is with me, it is possible to know peace wherever I am.

Without using mental gymnastics and arbitrarily selecting data, I can't construct a self-evident case that God is present. So unless I remain conscious, I reflexively drift back into acting as if I am alone and thinking as if my ideas are private. Nevertheless, external experience has to be given meaning, because each individual has a different take on the same food, fog, music, election, time of day, or lizard. This means that the day I *experience* is created by my mental state, which can acknowledge either nothing greater and more important than "me," or it can acknowledge the kingdom of heaven.

109

It never stops being now.

The journey back to God is the journey back to
now. To ascend into heaven is to sink so deeply into
now that we lose interest in past regrets and anxious
anticipations. But I make this so complicated.
"Should I plan for dinner; should I apologize for
what I said yesterday; should I make out a will . . .?"
To think about what it means to be in the present is
not to be in the present. Little children are so
unsophisticated that they run around, giggle, stare
at strangers, taste rocks, and just altogether have
way too much fun. They're so clueless, they
don't even know they have mastered advanced
metaphysical concepts and mystical techniques.
Today, I too will practice being clueless.

110

"I am finally flexible," will be my affirmation for today.

Our life makes contact with us at the point known as now. That is the place where it breaks out of time and into reality. Our real life span is composed of the number of nows we experience, and its quality is determined by how attentively we respond to the present. Except when we were children, most of us have not had a glimpse of our life in a long time. This is another way of saying that most of us need to learn how to relax, and nothing is learned without practice.

III

An untried moment
is an unlit candle.

Our mistrust of what we will find there keeps us from seeking the steadier ground and brighter vision offered by the present. We think of now as a place of boredom and tedium or of shocking pain that brings us back to our senses. So it requires a leap in faith just to *try* to settle into a lovingly illuminated quietness. This taste of divine peace, even if sustained, will not shield us from bad luck or unfair twists of fate. It operates on a different level of experience, but one that is definitely worth pursuing. The light from just one moment of stillness is instantly shared with others and permanently stored within us.

112

"Be not afraid" can only be practiced now.

My fear of the present—which is exhibited in my unwillingness to stop, to be present, and to truly do what I am doing—either holds me back from opportunities to make myself happy or hurries me beyond them.

113

Connection and fear cannot be experienced together.

If the ocean were pure mind and I were a wave, I would be in terror if I tried to separate myself from the substance that made me. What is a wave without water, and what is a mind without love?

114

A generous gesture
is never made alone.

Angels surround us and lift us up each time we
express our better nature. Let me imagine a world
I would truly like to be part of, because my efforts
to be happy, kind, and whole are helping to bring
it about.

115

True righteousness is a path of unlimited options.

The path to God is "straight" because it doesn't veer into limitation. It is "narrow" because it is completely pure. Thus it leads to ever-increasing freedom. There is a great difference between "being right" in opposition to others and maintaining a quiet inner sense of right-mindedness, which includes others. If I abandon my personal sense of right and wrong just because it's not the standard by which others live, I betray myself and so become an enemy to my own substance. The paradox of right and wrong is that although life is not righteous, I can make peace with my life only through righteousness.

116

Giving a spiritual gift
proves to my mind
that I already have it.

I forfeit all spiritual gifts the instant I stop
extending them to others. Any sense of discontent or
emptiness that I may experience today will indicate
the precise gift I must give to those around me.
I "receive" spiritual gifts only by giving them away.

117

The moment before and after a miracle is no less miraculous.

Love works miracles. Yet what do I choose to emphasize—the miracle or the Love? If I shift my attention to the miracle, I look away from its Cause. What happened may be wonderful indeed, yet Love is still present, still here, still holding me and everyone in beauty.

118

This day is blessed.

Because God encircles it and flows softly through it, my heart beats gently. My eyes are comforted by God's restful presence. My feet walk on the path prepared by God, and my hand holds God's in peace.

119

I am as God created me.

Your yearning for good is God's own voice. Your sense of purpose is God's own will. Within your kindness and devotion is God's love. What could you be that God is not?

120

The mind can ruminate,
but it can also relax and smile.

Surely it takes less effort for me to relax, open
up, and release old hurts and gnawing anxieties
than it does to continue gripping them tightly.
Concentration can be focused on letting go as easily
as on nurturing grievances and feeding apprehensions.

121

My mind, which is a gift from God, will never die. It is my responsibility and in my care forever.

Ego desires often come with a sense of urgency, as if the present moment will soon end: "Do it now" (before you come to your senses). "Just do it" (before your conscience kicks in). I am free to misuse my mind, but the lesson will be repeated until it is learned. Willfulness is not a happy approach to life. Yet if I pause long enough to experience sanity, not only do I rest from misery but I also give a measure of rest to an unquiet world, which has waited far too long for its human family to notice it.

122

From my peaceful mind,
I will speak gently
to the fearful part of me.

Monitor your willingness, and each time you feel
strong enough, put aside the evidence of your guilt
and the hopelessness of your condition. Quietly let
fear pass from your mind. Be still and remember
that God cannot lose sight of the beauty and
strength placed in your heart before time began.
You do not belong to your ego. You belong to God.

123

Spiritual growth is merely learning what makes us happy.

There is no greater deterrence to our progress than the suspicion that we are being asked to do more than we can and to give up things that we want. The path to God is not a burden, and the kingdom of heaven, which is all things limitless and good, is not reached through sacrifice. We are simply asked to trust, to love, and to be happy.

124

I am not healed alone.

Our potential as a healer has no point beyond which it can't go. To be kind to those around us and devote ourselves to their peace will do far more than make us happy. It will help release the world from pain and begin turning hell into heaven for every living thing.

125

Simply being happy
includes within it all spiritual effort
and all divine potential.

Be happy, and gently release your mind from what
makes you unhappy. That is the ancient secret; the
inner teaching; the lost knowledge; the message
of the still, quiet voice; the only wisdom ever to
be attained.

126

Everything I do matters.

There are no decisions without consequences. Each day I have a thousand opportunities to look and think with comfort, to understand rather than attack, to be human rather than right, to be whole rather than destructive. Every circumstance offers me a chance to side with my strength instead of my weaknesses, my peace instead of my fears, my destiny instead of my digressions into misery. And each small decision I make has its effect on my loved ones.

127

There is only one kind of love—
the uncalculating kind.

Love is simply the desire that those around me experience happiness, peace, and fulfillment. But it's not part of that desire that I must receive credit for the efforts I make or that my motives must be interpreted accurately. The desire for credit is unmitigated ego. Love is the willingness for each individual to find his or her own way and the trust that Something wiser than us is watching over us.

128

A gentle vision makes a gentler world through which to walk.

Judgmental people are obviously unhappy, but why do I find that insight so difficult to apply to my own judgments? What do I think is so desirable about dislike and ill will? Do I believe they make me superior? Or that they give me an advantage over nice people? Or that they will lead to a satisfying measure of revenge? Let me at least acknowledge that I remain stirred up and in distress as long as I hold a grudge. Let me also admit that I alone must feed a grievance in order to keep it alive.

129

If today I set all things free
to be as they are,
the earth can't help but dance,
and my heart dance with it.

If the world expressed Oneness, it would be
unrecognizable and no longer the world. It is a
place of friction and war, even on a molecular level.
Everything is separate. Everything has its own
agenda. I can accept this or I can wish it weren't so.
Acceptance allows me to be in the world but not
defined by it. A judgmental attitude puts me at odds
with everybody and everything, but an accepting
attitude allows the Beauty within me to become part
of my experience.

130

I already know enough.

Everyone knows enough to be a good friend,
a tolerant and helpful partner, a loving mother or
father, a considerate customer, a fair and honorable
boss. It really doesn't matter what I don't know if
I will apply all that I do know this instant. Just one
spiritual concept, practiced consistently, is enough.
The golden rule is an example of a safe substitute
for any moral philosophy, religion, or metaphysical
system on earth. But will I practice it today?

131

My behavior *reflects*
my state of mind.
My mind, not my behavior,
is the appropriate focus.

Trying to use mental sentences to change my
behavior is like standing before my shadow and
commanding it to move. It's not the words I think
but the overall motive I have that characterizes
my effect on others and myself. When I focus only
on controlling behavior, I relinquish the goal of
a consistent mental state. I can strive for inner
consistency or outer consistency, but not both.
How whole I am mentally determines how intu-
itive I am about other people and how sensitive
I am to their needs, as well as to my own.

132

I am not a victim of my childhood.

The divine has no interest in interpreting childhood scenes of misery and imposing them on the present. What once happened is not responsible for what is happening now—I alone am responsible, because I exist in the present. Do I want healing and wholeness, or do I want to continue justifying my mistakes? My ego is already formed, but whether to express it is my own choice.

133

Let the comments I make come from my heart, not my "honesty."

The ego is always creating symbols of defeat, just so it can tell itself it was in a fight. Its claim to reality is, "I oppose therefore I am." No wonder we often come away from conversations, even with friends, feeling slightly disappointed and dissatisfied. I delude myself if I think that I am communicating simply because I am literal. No two individuals' emotions are identical. On that level there is no joining. Only degrees of separateness can be expressed. Something deeper than "honestly" broadcasting my superficial thoughts and feelings is needed if I am to achieve a real connection with another person.

134

The one meaningful choice we have
is whether to receive our life
as a gift or to judge and fight it
every step of the way.

I keep trying to get the details of my life right. I
believe I have control of most of it and there are just
a few things left I need to master. Maybe it's a nagging
health problem, not enough money, something about
my appearance, or someone's annoying habit. But
even if I make progress with those, other things fall
apart. Yet I stubbornly refuse to acknowledge the
overall pattern. My distress is not coming from the
current areas of my life that are not to my liking, but
from my preoccupation with those areas. I believe
that my life is perfectible, but no one ever gets it all
under control.

135

The world doesn't work.
Trying to make it work is
the root of my distress.

No matter what circumstance I find myself in,
my ego is never entirely at peace. If I could change
"just this one thing" about the situation, it would
be acceptable. But that assumes everything else will
remain the same. If one thing changes, the situation
as a whole must change, because its very meaning
depends on contrast and comparison. So after I
change "this one thing," something new arises that
is equally preoccupying. This dynamic will end only
when I stop making control my priority.

136

Tolerance and understanding transcend "right and wrong."

There can be no absolute right or wrong in a world of individuals. Reality is what reality is. Whatever it may be, it is so vast that no one person sees it all. There could be no more relationship standoffs if simply this much were realized: We are all looking at the same immense reality—and each of us is seeing *something*. When I reject another person's point of view completely, I am saying that he or she is not looking at anything. I already know what I have to say. Wouldn't it at least be more *interesting* to hear what they have to say?

137

Any attitude, technique,
or philosophy helpful
to another person
deserves my support.

The question isn't whether I believe in another
individual's approach or would choose it for myself.
The question is whether that approach affirms life.
I should be encouraging and supportive of any idea,
therapy, or procedure that allows someone to let go
of misery. Today I will challenge the unloving
thoughts that cross my mind about other people's
approaches to healing, worshiping, or just living
everyday life.

138

All I can do
is try my best.

"All you can do is the best you can." This simple acknowledgment releases unnecessary anxiety over how much needs to be accomplished and returns my mind to the only time in which anything can be done. "We can always do better" does not actually conflict with the peaceful acknowledgement that "we will accomplish what we will accomplish." It simply states that potential has no limits. But no matter what the form, anxiety over quantitative goals is not accomplishment.

139

Peace dissolves
the grip of time.

The busy mind is focused on how much is accomplished in time. The peaceful mind is focused on how much of the timeless is experienced this instant.

140

Do I want the question,
or do I want the answer?

I am not resting in Love's gentle arms while I am questioning how the arms got there or demanding to know why they would want to comfort *me*.

141

By judging,
I surrender self-control.

When I decide to judge, I also decide to shift my power to the object of my attack. And although I may start by judging one thing only, by believing that even a single judgment is justified, I affirm the validity of the entire process of judging. In that instant I become a keyboard upon which any individual or event can sound out the notes of my personal history. Now I am a passive instrument through which anyone and anything can play my preprogrammed tune—even though no one else can hear it.

142

Anxiety does not improve relationships.

Anxiously trying to please is another way of trying
to change someone. It also makes me a victim.
I believe that I can't accept their present attitude
toward me. And I think that acceptance is the
enemy. But acceptance doesn't make me more
vulnerable since it does not preclude a change of
heart; it precludes remaining in conflict.

143

Disagreements cannot diminish love.

To the ego part of us, love is agreement. "If you really loved me, you would agree with my beliefs, prefer what I prefer, and support my decisions." But true love is seeing each other clearly and accepting each other as we are. Real love recognizes that there are always disagreements between personalities, and it finds them interesting rather than jolting.

144

The Voice within all hearts is the same.

If the light within us allows us to see the spiritual, it must also provide the gentle recognition of what guides us all. It shines softly on the path we walk and reveals how blessed we are to travel together. Arguments over what to call this Beneficence betray the very nature of the guidance. It is enough to trust that what speaks within one heart, speaks within the hearts of everyone.

145

Only by loving can I feel
and have the experience
of *being* loved.

A loving mind is blessed even as it blesses. But if I
look to see if I am being loved, for that instant it is
impossible for me to love. Love is not a matter of
compromise and reciprocity. It is wholly one-sided,
inclusive, and complete.

146

I am not being "nice" if I am conflicted about it.

If there is misgiving in the giving, the gift is not yet mine to give. If I am conflicted about why I am doing something for someone, conflict is my dominant gift.

147

My state of mind is all I truly give to another.

If I give a concept, all that is received is a concept. If I give time, it runs out. If I give objects or money, they can be misused or misinterpreted. Money, objects, concepts, and time can be powerful symbols of the divine, but only if they come from love.

148

What I see
is what I get.

Sight is a literal extension of our self. A gentle vision extends a power as real as its object and transforms it into its own nature. In my presence you become the part of my heart that I have set free.

149

To learn something new, I have to resign as my own teacher.

Life doesn't select particular lessons for me to identify and learn. Nor does it whisper instructions that I must hear and interpret correctly. All it asks is that I not be my own self-appointed guru. Today I will practice making no assumptions and drawing no conclusions. If I do this, Life itself will take care of everything else.

150

The voice of the past
is not the voice of God.

For me to take from the countless contradictory
experiences I have had and emphasize only a certain
type of experience, and then install it as a guide
for future action, is not self-trust, but a lack of it.
I have never known anyone who had a completely
balanced approach to life. Everyone overemphasizes
something. Surely I'm not the exception! Our past
self is in the past; our present self is in the present,
and only in the present can it be trusted.

151

Spiritual emotions are limitless and ever present. Ego emotions are limited and bound to the past.

The Sermon on the Mount removes all qualifications from the old virtues. A virtue is pure and sincere only if it has no exceptions. I certainly should consider whether at times it is appropriate to act happy, to behave affectionately, or to profess my faith. But within the heart, love, happiness, and faith require no restraint.

152

Judging judgmentalness is still judging.

How can I presume to block the way of love by weighing which of God's children is deserving and which is not? Anyone is free to break my spiritual rules. If in the name of my faith I say they are not, that is merely judging in order to stop judging.

153

Forgiveness is spontaneous and does not require "good judgment."

Never is it best to consider whether to forgive. Never is it best to wait to see if someone else is doing his or her part. Forgiveness is an act of self-preservation and should be an instinctual response to the damage anger is doing to my own mind.

154

To forgive is to reconnect with God.

Anger, irritation, dislike, disapproval, hatred, and the like break my connection with Love. Forgiveness is a proactive acknowledgment that I would rather have that connection than be "right" about another person. Hesitating to reconnect only hurts *me*.

155

Happiness begins with increased awareness of others.

Pet owners who ask the question, "What does this animal's behavior say about me?" are capable of insensitivity and sometimes cruelty toward their pet. For example, they may demand that a dog be absolutely obedient and loyal to them yet see no reason why they should have a lifelong commitment to the dog. Likewise, I am acutely aware of other people's attitudes toward me, yet I am not consistently conscious of my attitude toward them.

156

Love sees
without interpretation.

Most of the time I don't truly see other people.
I see them in relationship to me. I first look at
myself, then at the other person. Real love removes
comparisons from the process and sees others
directly. It doesn't filter what another person does
through the ego's perennial question, "How do
I feel about that?" It bypasses the distorting lens of
my temporary needs and ever-shifting self-image
and sees other individuals from within *them*.

157

The egos I encounter today
do not have to affect
my sense of self.

In a group setting, or in a one-to-one exchange,
I should acknowledge the intuitions and impressions
that I have. However, if I disturb this process by also
ranking myself against the characteristics I see and
the facts I learn about other people, my sense of self
is immediately altered, because I am then making
the egos of those around me part of who I think
I am.

158

Take others into your heart, not into your self-esteem.

The part of me that is connected to others and to the divine speaks directly to my mind. It informs me of who I am, where I am, and Who is with me. The ego tries to find some way to turn all situations into praise for itself, including problems and failures. But true self-esteem is built and sustained through connection with our Source. Thus low self-esteem is not a problem of insufficient inner cheerleading.

159

Oneness is the experience: "Here is someone I know."

It's impossible to believe that another person is different from me yet withhold assigning a value to those differences. I will be judgmental of myself, or of the other, if differences are all I focus on. How personalities contrast is spiritually unimportant. Oneness is feeling and seeing myself in another. It is relaxing my mind and letting go of the importance I place on my superficial identity.

160

Until I pause and feel my wholeness, I will continue searching.

Whether wealth, reputation, respect, a more exciting lover, an ostentatious car, or "buns of steel," nothing that anyone acquires satisfies them for long. Only by mistrusting that God has filled us with a spirit that is innocent, whole, and abundant can we doom ourselves to walk down every alley, looking under every piece of junk and litter, searching for some undefined something that has never been found by anyone.

161

Which voice am I listening to this instant?

Everyone hears and follows inner guidance. The question is which voice do we hear? The answer is, the one we want to hear. Do I want to hear the voice of my past conditioning, which is conflicted, often exciting, and always full of false promise? Or do I want to hear the peaceful voice of the present and be whole? My heartfelt answer to this question—and not simply the act of listening—determines what I hear.

162

Because God is love,
I am never alone.

Regardless of what spiritual beliefs they profess, most people believe they are alone. They think, act, and pray as if they are alone. This is simple denial that Love exists. It is a misperception that spills on everything in the world they see, and it blocks the experience of peace.

163

Anxiety signals
how I am using my mind.

It's not our lack of faith, not what we *don't* believe, but what we do believe, that causes anxiety. The only possible outcome of thinking there is nothing in the universe that has unshakable confidence in me, and in whose presence I am always welcomed, is fear.

164

Ego emotions are manufactured by thoughts.

Fighting ego emotions is a losing battle, but awareness of the thoughts that produce them allows me to stop being a victim. Small children are controlled—all their ideas, movements, and emotions—by the thought that there might be a monster under the bed. Hearing their parents say, "There are no monsters," does not lessen the power of the thought. Yet if they turn on a light and look under the bed, they take responsibility for their mind and reclaim control of it. Likewise, telling myself that a feeling of sadness, fear, anger, or loneliness is unreasonable will not stop the feeling. Yet if I look closely at the particular thought under the emotion, I loosen its grip.

165

Fear of stillness is the desire to remain confused.

The belief that I am alone is at the core of my feelings of being put upon, overwhelmed, depressed, or confused. God's commitment to me doesn't need arguing or defending. But my belief that I am alone does need close examination and questioning. "Why do I continue to believe that I am alone when just a few moments of stillness shows me that I am not?" This question should not be a self-accusation, but a genuine inquiry.

166

I see the reality that most interests me.

Seeing the divine is a matter of focus. It is not that difficult to find because it's everywhere I look. But the images of malice, war, superficiality, death, insensitivity, and disease are also everywhere I look. My deeper interest determines which "reality" dominates my mind and the one I pass on to others.

167

How I use my mind determines my experience.

Dwell not on what is cruel, chaotic, or discouraging. Dwell not on things of smallness: little slights and petty worries. See the ego clearly, but don't become preoccupied. Dwell instead on gentle beauty, on the sound of laughter, on gestures of kindness, on signs of patience and forbearance. Dwell on oneness and wholeness. Dwell only on what can be extended and shared.

168

All inner shifts are reflected outward.

If I am thinking defensively about even one person, my entire mind is in a defensive mode. Attack, no matter what the form, can't be compartmentalized. And any mind at war with the people and memories that inhabit it, reproduces this war within every outward situation and relationship. Whereas a mind that is united and quiet reproduces simplicity and peace.

169

The images my mind keeps returning to inform me of what I rely on.

There are no purely random thoughts and I should remain aware of the drift of my thinking. To resent, to long for, or to regret, is to place my trust in the wrong reality. I adopt a set of laws that are wholly unlike divine law. In this way I live in a purgatory of my own making. Although this choice doesn't control the experience other people have, I can't help but offer them a more difficult life.

170

Whenever I stumble, let my response be to wait in stillness on my God.

Let me make gentleness and mental quietness my standard, my protection, and my goal. Let me not chew on the ego's meatless bones: what someone meant by something they said. How hopelessly incompetent I am. How unfair life is. How misunderstood I am by my family. How impossible spiritual attainment is. Let me instead practice the Answer, which is stillness of mind, connection with others, and trust in God.

171

If I will release it, my mind can gently rise above chaos.

Because its nature is to soar in freedom and enter the place of peace effortlessly, today I will picture my mind as a beautiful and buoyant balloon, and I will release it to the divine. Now it is chained to a world that is old and tired, where we have grown weary of fractured lives and relationships, of pointless triumphs and short-lived accomplishments, of eventual loss and inevitable endings. Today it is within my power to release my mind and let it soar above separation and pain. Each time I practice this, my self-imposed chains become weaker and my happiness more certain.

172

I will not resist my happiness.

Love, which contains no aggression, flows through anyone who does not resist it. Today I am willing to fulfill the function Love has assigned me. I am willing to be and to feel like the image and likeness of God.

173

Forgiveness is the willingness to be happy.

I won't ask God to help me forgive because forgiveness occurs when I want it to. It is my desire to release another person from my decisions about them. I forgive the instant I want to, the instant I grow weary of a miserable state of mind. It's my responsibility to change my mind, not God's. Asking God to help me with this is just the decision to procrastinate a while longer and remain a victim of what I alone am doing to myself. God won't force me to desire what I don't wholly desire.

174

Do I want to be guilty or do I want to be innocent?

Forgiveness of myself can only come from wholeness, and wholeness can only come from welcoming the fact that I am joined with others and with God. To be realized, the desire to experience oneness must be taken into each mental encounter and outward contact. It must be actively sought, or else I will mindlessly concede my guilt to my ego.

175

What I believe I am
is what I give to another.

What comes from within me informs me of what
I am, and I will believe that it's me because it is the
proof I myself have provided. When I am good,
I feel my inherent goodness and silently call to the
goodness in others. But if I extend conflict, then
I am alone and call to the loneliness in others.

176

Acknowledging inner conflict is the first step to making better decisions.

In thinking of things I am worried about or of things I want changed, if I ask myself, "What would I like to happen?" the first few outcomes that come to mind are often superficial. But if I keep asking, "What else would I like to happen?" my desires often deepen. Yet as they do, they also start to conflict with the earlier desires. Recognizing the contrasting outcomes that I think I want, gives me the option of choosing what part of me I wish to be more of. In this way, conflict can be well used.

177

Until I am consistently honest with myself, I will never know consistent peace.

Awareness means putting all my cards on the table; that is, calling forth all my impulses—negative and positive. Awareness is conscious acknowledgment of everything I believe about myself and others— even the parts that make me uneasy. Being verbally honest is sometimes kind and often unkind, but being honest with myself is always an act of love and fundamental to progress.

178

I am never a victim of my thoughts unless I want to be.

I can choose to overlook my ego thoughts and say I'm not really responsible because I lack awareness. Or I can acknowledge these thoughts yet choose to be destructive anyway "because the temptation is just too great." But there is never total unawareness. No "hardwiring," "basic nature," or "inner demons" can force me to betray my higher mind. However I may justify betrayal of myself or others, I alone choose to be a victim of my thoughts.

179

I put myself
in a position of weakness
when I cherish a grievance.

When I hold onto resentment or bitterness, I can't help but see myself as a victim, because I have put someone else in control. And as long as I think of myself as a victim, I have nothing but weakness to extend to others. Thus a victim self-image is not only damaging to me but to the people I love.

180

Unhappiness requires a past.
Happiness needs only this instant.

Living in the present is a form of taking responsibility
because it removes what I depend on to justify my
unhappiness. It puts my mind back into my own
hands. The past is plainly visible in the facial
expressions of most adults. Whereas the faces of
little children are usually clear and free of the past.

181

My past is not present unless I draw it into my mind.

If I believe I am damaged from what my parents did or failed to do, then I am justified in acting out the same old patterns. "I am not responsible for this character failing because of what was done to me." But nothing is being done to me this instant. I am responsible for how I am now because I alone decide to recall and honor the damage.

182

There are no discrete attacks.
I can't love myself
while judging another.

Blame makes the object of my attack the driving
force of my thinking. I focus on fracture and
division and thereby split my power into opposing
attitudes. It's impossible to blame without also
feeling guilty. Even as I attack the other individual,
I am compelled to attack myself. My mind tries
to hold onto two identities—one innocent, one
guilty—but in order to sustain both, it is forced
to shuttle between the two. I can't blame without
becoming a blamer. Yet if I simply decline to blame,
my mind returns to its inherent wholeness.

183

A state of longing
blocks the experience of wholeness.

A life well lived is not consumed with one futile
search after another—as all searches for what
I believe I don't have must be. A life well lived is
consumed with present discovering and present
finding. It is a movable banquet, a deep and
ongoing commemoration of what I possess in
Truth, regardless of my circumstances or the
vagaries of fate.

Acknowledging my problems is a positive sign of willingness. It is not negative thinking.

The journey toward perfection is, by definition, a path of imperfection. Each step is a slight correction of the faulty direction in which I am heading. I have a right to many things, but a life without problems is not one of them.

185

Peace and perfection cannot be found in the body.

Ask not of illness what spiritual mistake you made. Ask not what your accident means. Look not for order in chaos. Look not for meaning in the meaningless. Why do I keep demanding of my body what it is incapable of giving? What can be gained from judging myself for being physically vulnerable? God is the one thing in the universe that has meaning, and accident, disease, and tragedy are not a part of God.

186

Freedom is
a quiet state of mind.

Stillness is the beginning step in freeing the mind of useless battles. Stillness is often associated with physical quietness and restricted activity, but the effort I must make is to carry inner calmness into each small task. In this way, I establish a theme of freedom that runs continuously through my day regardless how loud or hectic it may become.

187

Wholeness is first seen in others before it is felt within.

Our vision has been shattered, but not the spiritual truth of our wholeness. Each individual we encounter appears to hold a lost piece of us. It joins with us the instant it is recognized. But only a calm and innocent vision can see it.

188

To bring healing to my relationships,
I will remember that God is joy.

Because minds are joined, just one happy, restful
purpose will of itself extend throughout all areas
of my relationships. Lightheartedness is not a
superficial quality. I will begin with an easy goodwill
toward the one who is before me now, and all my
other relationships will benefit.

189

Love cannot be restrained.

Love starts as special love for one person, yet because it is love, it soon starts to expand. Likewise, it isn't possible to focus attack thoughts and thereby block their spread. If I am truly accepting of just one person, I become accepting of all people. Yet if I judge a single individual, I begin poisoning all my relationships.

190

In God
there are no needs.

The unanticipated and uncontrollable ways that life
so often plays out make it clear that I don't know
what is good for me or even what I truly want. To
decide what I need and then ask God to provide
it, is at best partial trust. By trusting God fully,
I discover that my needs are already answered.

191

The ego speaks first, but in stillness I will listen for the voice of sanity.

In everything we do, our ego has its own agenda, and its voice is always present. When we started a spiritual path, our ego did also. On all occasions our mind contains some conflict, and we can look back on any decision we made and remember our ego motivation, because the ego did, in fact, speak. That is why *any* relationship can be reinterpreted as having started negatively, even though at the time we may have actually followed the peace of our hearts. Today I will be aware of both voices within me and, even as I acknowledge my ego motivation, I will consciously choose the voice of sanity instead.

192

So that I may remain open, I will practice divine doubt.

It's natural and healthy to doubt ourselves. Those who do not doubt, easily mislead themselves. It's also quite difficult to feel connection with individuals who are rigid in their beliefs. My most insensitive mistakes have come when I was certain I was right. Doubt, when properly used, keeps me humble, balanced, and eager for God's continuing guidance.

193

To accept responsibility
for everything I think and do—
but guilt for nothing already corrected—
is humility true and pure.

A general uneasiness, a pang of conscience, or a sudden stab of anxiety can be a useful indicator that I am not being honest with myself. First, I must acknowledge what I am not facing. Next, I must act to correct it, even if this can only be done mentally. Only then can I safely reject feelings of guilt.

194

If I compare myself spiritually
to another, I see oneness.
But if I compare my ego to theirs,
I do not see.

We each have different versions of illness and
physical incapacity. Likewise, our personalities,
none of which are perfect, are flawed in individual
ways. No matter what aspect of a person is being
considered, whether teacher or student, "old soul"
or "new," believer or nonbeliever, one individual is
no more divine than another. To believe we are
superior because we are more likeable, better
looking, "have money," have children, or are called
"master" or "advanced" within a spiritual discipline,
is self-delusion and a complete block to peace.

195

Today I will acknowledge the obvious.

I can bless my body far more effortlessly than I can misuse it. It is easier to like my partner, my child, or my friend than to dislike them. It takes less work to feel connected than to feel superior. It is more difficult to make things difficult.

196

Forgiveness is always possible— in the present.

To forgive someone completely and forever may seem unworkable. But can't I forgive this person for the space of a single breath? Can't I hold the image of this person in my mind for just one instant while still remaining whole and at peace? Then let me practice at least this much.

197

To forgive another
I must first be honest with myself.

Very often trying to forgive feels like trying to change reality. But forgiveness is simply returning to peace. If I am stirred up about someone, my purpose is not to squelch my troubled mind. It is to return my attention to my peaceful mind, where nothing needs to be done or undone. To do this, I have the option of going to the source of the disturbance and surrounding in light the troubled image that I hold of the other person. This doesn't dishonestly condone what the individual did; it honestly addresses the part I am playing in my own mental distress.

198

Let me not be afraid
to relax and be happy.
I can't put myself in jeopardy
by resting a moment in God.

When I'm in the grip of my ego—whether angry,
discouraged, afraid, jealous, judgmental, or any
number of other such attitudes—I still have the
option of pausing and remembering that God wants
me to be happy and has provided a way for that
to happen. Simply remembering God renews my
connection with the place where I am already whole.

199

Remain in the present.
Walk in peace.
Love and laugh easily.
What more is there to do than this?

God is one; that is how simple God is. Truth is true;
that is how simple reality is. Love is love; that is
how simple what I have to do is.

200

God knows the question before I ask.

Do I really think God needs my explanation?
Simply by deciding to relax into my better nature,
and to rest there happily, I put myself into the care
of the most benevolent power there is. God doesn't
have to provide the answer; God is the answer.

201

What I want from you
is what I deny I have.

To want something from another is to utterly misunderstand their role in our happiness. Other people are our opportunity to extend what we *are*.

202

To listen with peace transforms discord into melody.

Most people assume that in a loving relationship, individuals are alike and have matching interests and opinions. Yet in reality, there are no well-matched couples or completely compatible friends. On a personality level, individuals differ in all respects and cannot be made identical. Whether the areas of agreement seem to be about food, weather, finances, entertainment, sports, parenting, or politics, look closely enough and you see separate attitudes about every detail. Yet none of this matters if both people see the differences clearly, accept the differences fully, and continue to practice peace.

203

Freedom, like all spiritual treasures,
must first be given
before it is received.

People who are lifelong friends or inseparable
partners invariably give each other enormous
freedom to be themselves. The reward is that they
become comfortable with who *they* are as well.

204

Comfort with myself, not war with myself, is the agent for change.

The world believes that if something needs to change, something more needs to be done. It believes that peace occurs when we are preemptive, that personal change occurs when we are proactive, and that love is a matter of winning and losing. But real change comes from letting go of what I think has to be changed. It may or may not involve increased activity, but it always involves becoming inwardly calm and quietly listening.

205

Do I want to be my ego, or do I want to be my self?

What at first appears to be personal transformation is in fact personal acceptance. This never entails ego acquiescence but rather acceptance of the deeper self, which is the connected self. Thus acceptance is not an insular or self-centered act. It is a willingness to allow the old boundaries of my identity to dissolve.

206

If I try to force a picture of oneness, I destroy oneness.

Parents who force their kids to participate in dinner conversation and individuals who force their partners to say, "I love you," make a similar mistake. They value the appearance of oneness more than oneness. Just as I will never become more peaceful by trying to make my personality *appear* more peaceful, I will never get someone to love me by trying to make them act more lovingly.

207

The external can't be made to reflect the spiritual.

In the world, there has never been a symbol of eternal, unchanging oneness. There has never been a moment of peace that began and never ended. If I am to find oneness and peace, it will be within the consistency of my own heart.

208

Oneness does not see degrees of inequality.

The sum of the things we own, the superior state of our health, the many years we live, or the number of spiritual concepts we accumulate do not attest to our spiritual advancement any more than loss or scarcity adds respectability to the body that experiences it. Within a mindset of oneness, versions of inequality are not ranked. In fact, they are not even perceived as meaningful.

209

Until I take the time
to see them clearly,
I will continue to fall
into the same behavioral traps.

The ego mind is always up to something. Consequently, the body usually does what it does not need to be doing now. For instance, individuals often start projects and couples begin discussing issues when they are tired and should be getting ready for bed. To have any hope of a simpler life, I must become more conscious of what I am doing with my thoughts this instant. This kind of awareness requires more practice than I have previously cared to admit. But the reward is release from my tired old patterns and mistakes.

210

To become aware of God,
first I must become aware of what
I find more interesting than God.

Around me are billions of separate details.
Accompanying these potential perceptions is an
array of past experiences that I could use as reference
points to give any detail meaning. Thus the day
I experience is created from what I choose to look
at and how I decide to interpret it. Yet in the back-
ground of all things separate there is a single, divine
Truth and one, whole embracing experience. I need to
be aware of what in particular I find more compelling
than God. Every version of the present moment that
is not dominated by a calm, kind attitude is devoid of
real meaning and doomed to be unsatisfying.

211

Let me not be afraid to look,
to be aware,
and to be deeply honest
with myself.

We have all encountered individuals who seemed unaware of their bad breath or body odor. More importantly, perhaps everyone we know seems oblivious to at least one or two aspects of their egos. Is it possible that I am the one exception, the one person who in no way functions unconsciously? Obviously not. How then can a reluctance to search for the precise ways I think destructively make me less destructive? How can I correct a failing if I don't acknowledge it in the first place? To be "positive" is to be whole, not to be naïve.

212

Whose dwelling is without dust?
Whose mind is without litter?

Actively and persistently searching out my mental
mistakes does not make my mind *more* negative—
because these are mistakes I was already making.
Nonetheless, it is pointless to dwell on garbage.
It merely needs to be identified and thrown out.

213

Because the world is a place of war,
the path of peace
must be intentionally practiced.

The world calls to our ego, and unless we are
vigilant, we answer the call daily. Nothing is gained
without study and practice. Thus we need a plan,
and the plan must be consciously followed. Yet once
we are thoroughly acquainted with our ego, we can
look past it to the gentler side of ourselves. Now the
place of peace is not so easily lost, because we know
exactly how we arrived there. We also know how we
blocked our perception of peace before and are alert
to any sign that we are about to block it again.

214

When I am happy,
I don't need to
look over my shoulder.

The reason to examine nothingness is to see that it is nothing. Nonsense must be recognized as nonsense, but once recognized, it can be forgotten. It will not come back to bite us, because its only effects were the ones we ourselves created. To those standing in the light, darkness is no threat.

215

Worrying does not protect me.
Intuition is born of peace.

Keeping our guard up has come to mean keeping
our mind focused on our archive of fears, as if the
universe has a conscience and if it sees that we aren't
receiving our quota of hardships, it soon will set
the balance right. Yet in every life a little sunshine
must fall. This is normal, so I don't need to sweat it.
Nor do I need to doubt that there is a blessing that
transcends occasional good luck and favorable
circumstances. That which is greater than us is
greater in all respects, including unwavering kindness, eternal commitment, and unconditional love.

216

God's love is trustworthy and unchanging.

The Psalmist writes, "If I make my bed in hell, behold, Thou art there. . . . Even there shall thy hand lead me and thy right hand shall hold me." Hell perceived clearly is hell destroyed, and our need to fear it or remember it never returns. Be therefore at peace. I can *believe* in a place outside of Everywhere, but fear cannot add to the limitless. Whether I choose to experience it now or later, I never left God's embrace.

217

Home is found in my heart,
where God placed it. Thus opening
my heart expands my home.

To most adults, the present moment seems small, dull,
and quite confining. The world around them trumpets
future dreams and past accomplishments. Nothing
seems important that doesn't relate to what once was
or soon will be. An accomplishment has no meaning
if no one remembers it. An award would have no
significance if no one reacted in the following days.
Yet children and pets teach a different approach to the
present. Little kids don't like long talks about what
happened earlier. Nor do they find discussions of what
might occur tomorrow very interesting. Most of them
still feel a connection with the presence of divine joy.

218

Love completes
what Love begins.

We all could do a better job of lifting the burden from each others' shoulders, even though we know that love brought us together. Friends and family can be so exhausting. Usually we make life more difficult for each other, whereas love always makes life easier. Even though I have often approached relationships perversely, let me have a little faith that the power that brings us together can also complete the transaction. My part is not to bail out on the process.

219

Attack thoughts
shrink and harden my mind.

Disliking, disdaining, judging, and condemning
drain light and space from my mind. Letting go of
thoughts of separation releases my energy, expands
my mind, and simplifies my life. The only catch is
that when I take responsibility for my thoughts,
I now have no one to blame.

220

Commitment does not preclude
peace, and peace does not
preclude commitment.

Most of us think we are in situations we should not
have to accept and around people we should not
have to endure. Yet the life of every saint, prophet,
and master is a story of acceptance that endures and
endurance that accepts.

221

Embarrassment can block peace,
but it adds nothing to my life.

Embarrassment is shrunken perspective. There is always a lot more going on than we see or imagine. So there are worse approaches than trusting that God holds our hand and walks beside us. There are worse approaches than believing that we are each loved with a love so large that all our mistakes are washed clean. There are worse approaches than to walk forth in newness into a day drenched in light.

222

Being interested is a decision,
and what we love,
we find interesting.

Being interested in individuals is an essential part
of loving them. Become interested and you will
love. Love and you will become interested. Decide
that a person is not interesting and you will never
find a way to love them.

223

**If peace is my priority,
then I must protect my mind
from what poisons it.**

No matter how stirring the call to my autonomy,
any concept, teaching, book, or form of media that
enhances my sense of being set apart, that makes
me worry about the limits on other people's ability
to change, or that increases my suspicion of my
partner, my child, or other loved ones cannot lead
me to the kinds of relationships I long for. God
teaches love, not worry; certainty, not analysis;
oneness, not detachment; hope, not fear.

224

Communication is a function of empathy and can occur with or without words.

Only my ego asks, "What should I say?" My heart asks, "What do I choose to feel?" No matter the communication technique I use, if I feel separate from the person I am talking to, I may listen, but I will not hear. The mind can't pursue opposite goals at the same time. Feeling critical of myself and of the other person must be suspended, if only for the moment, in order to communicate effectively.

225

A still mind
is inherently tolerant.

Because minds are already joined, only a busy mind
can block communication. The ability to see another
person clearly springs from gentle tolerance, not
from scrutiny. Tolerance is the child of stillness.

226

Today I will judge no one by their behavior.

Appearances are merely a dream about you. They are not what I can see you actually are when I look within. Your cry to be understood and appreciated is not a futile gesture unless I focus only on your behavior. Today I will see you as you are deeply, not superficially, just as I would want others to see me.

227

The experience of oneness
is wordless and still.

Oneness is not reached for, but comfortably settled
into. There is a single Self, and worldly identities
are an illusion. If we look outside, we see a splintered reality. But if we look inside, we see the unity
of all living things.

228

Oneness is the willingness to think without fear.

If the differences between cultures, races, sexes, origins, and so on were taken to heart, the best any two friends or lovers could hope for would be an alliance, and alliances are always broken when a new alliance seems more interesting. But if the heart of God is the heart of everyone I encounter, only fear can block my experience of equality.

229

When I am defensive, I choose to protect the wrong self.

I can be defensive and contrast myself with others, or I can have a generous mind and be happy, but I can't be both happy and defensive. To sustain my worldly identity, walls must be erected and vigilantly maintained, but this comes at a high price: I no longer know who I am.

230

All differences dissolve
when I fall back
into my broader self.

It's not that I can somehow make myself see no
inequality. That wouldn't even be helpful, and
people who adopt this pretense often make the
person they are talking to feel disconnected. What
I can do is not take the differences I see to heart,
not make them more important than my deeper
sense that each individual is loved and valued
equally by God.

231

Never be afraid to expand the definition of who you are.

As I go through the day, I unquestionably have the option of carrying with me a sense of physical vulnerability and smallness; I can think of what I am not getting and who is to blame; I can imagine things the future may fail to provide; and I can feel guilty and afraid. But there is an alternative attitude. It is to relinquish the insane notion that everything needs to be controlled. It is to believe in the broader picture and the ultimate outcome. It is to relax and be at peace.

232

Since at our core we are the same,
understanding another person is
essentially an act of self-acceptance.

"Trying hard to understand" someone is the wrong
approach to the right goal. Understanding comes
from calmness and a quiet, steady vision, which are
impossible if I believe in a fractured reality. If
"my reality" is unique, understanding the whole is
precluded, because there is no whole. And yet, if
a single divine truth runs deep in everyone, understanding others is simply a matter of looking within
my own heart honestly.

233

The divine does not "test" us
or give us "trials"
before blessing us.

How could God increase pressure, expand the rules,
or set new demands if divine Love is changeless and
the peace of God is eternal? We know when we
are hearing the voice of God because the opposite
happens. Suddenly all the pressure is lifted, and we
feel loved just the way we are. This is also the gift
I must give those around me.

234

Today I will not rank the activities I engage in.

Almost any activity is inherently interesting. I can stick with my predetermined attitude about large gatherings, uninvited house guests, answering snail mail, waiting in line at the DMV, and a hundred other circumstances I have decided I don't like, or I can accept the situation I am in and look for ways to enjoy it. The only thing I have to lose is my self-righteousness.

235

God gave us our mind to make us happy.

We are free to misuse the gifts God gave us, or at least to imagine that we have that power. We can dream of a world where there is no real evidence of the divine, where all things live off the death of something else, and where everything, even the stars and their constellations, eventually end. But the smile of God, which knows no time, hasn't vanished simply because we fantasize it has. We are free to misuse our mind, but we can also use it kindly, peacefully, and generously, which allows us to experience its divine origin and partake of its true power.

236

Happiness is easy.
It's letting go of unhappiness
that's hard. We're willing to give up
everything but our misery.

A hundred times a day our love of happiness is cut
short by our even greater fear of it. A happy thought
is inevitably followed by a "realistic" one. If we find
ourselves laughing with abandon, singing in the shower,
or whistling loud enough to be overheard, for some
nagging reason we feel we must resume a "serious"
state of mind. And yet it's happiness that is truly practical and serious. It positively affects our mental and
physical health, our relationships with friends and
family, our job performance, not to mention our
relationship with God. Happiness connects us with
Reality; unhappiness disconnects us.

237

**I must become familiar with how
I make myself unhappy before
I can know consistent happiness.**

Even at a party, which is supposedly tailor-made to be
a here-and-now experience, I'm surprised how often
I mentally look around waiting for a better moment.
For a better person to talk to. For the time when
I can eat. For a break in the discussion. For the right
moment to leave. So, obviously, anticipations are a
killer. So are judgmental lines of thought. And the
desire to control. And certainly making comparisons—
how my present income, energy level, place of dwelling,
age, hair line, waist line, cultural awareness, degree of
peace, compare. There is clearly a universe of mental
mistakes that I passively condone. This must be stud-
ied until I am permanently alert to the consequence—
good or bad—of each line of thought.

238

Do not allow the body to reflect your attack thoughts.

The notion that the negativity of the ego should be outwardly expressed ("vented") comes from my assumption that if I "get it out," it is no longer "in." Whereas the opposite is true. When I allow my words (or my silence) to express my decision to attack, my negativity deepens and becomes more engrossing, and I stir up the other person as well. Now the problem is more complicated and takes on a life of its own. Spiritual damage control is acting with kindness even when I don't feel like it.

239

A watched mind never boils.

The first step to restoring happiness is, if it's boiling, put the lid on the ego so it doesn't splatter on other people. Now I have taken responsibility for my state of mind and can focus on what I alone can control. As long as I am in my ego, I am out of control. But once I allow my thoughts to settle down, I discover that the stillness I experience is already in control, because there is no conflict within it.

240

My ego chatters like a monkey,
but its thoughts fade in importance
when I am still.

My ego is like every other ego—it is capable of
almost any bizarre thought. I don't have to speak
"honestly" about these thoughts. In fact, they are
so random and contradictory it would be impossible
to voice them all without sounding like a babbling
idiot, which I often sound like anyway. Instead, if I
gently sink below all the chatter into my God-given,
God-sustained quietness, I become this other thing
that is not my ego.

241

Each moment of the day,
I decide the direction of my life.

Within our ego mind there are countless choices,
yet from the broader perspective of the divine, there
is only one decision to make. Most of my life I have
wandered aimlessly because I refused to admit that
I am always changing directions. The time has come
to decide between my peaceful mind and my busy
mind. There is no other meaningful choice.

242

To be right
is to be separate.

In God—that is, within happiness, love, and peace—
I am naturally myself and naturally bonded with
others. The effort required of me to be in God is
to let go of my decision to be right. Deciding to
be right is my attempt to separate myself from the
right-mindedness of God. It's also my attempt to
become a victim of the person I have made wrong.
And when I feel like a victim, I am at my most
destructive. All of this can be remedied by having
a little honest chat with myself.

243

The mind can focus either
on what it has or
what it thinks it doesn't have,
but it can't do both at once.

God's holy light is in us and all around us. In
quietness, may this light fill us completely and
gently shine away all desires and all attachments,
until, finally, our love excludes no one and our
mind no longer dreams of needs.

244

Desire is the root of suffering
because its focus
is on the absence of God.

When I let go of my old assumptions, I release
myself from desire. To be without assumptions
is to trust God. But I must then make no new
assumptions or else I will generate new desires.
When I have let go of everything—all assumptions
and all desires—I will be left with nothing but God.

245

I am in heaven or hell depending on what has my attention.

I stand before the kingdom of happiness but do not perceive it because my mind is stirred up. I have to "be here now" before I can open the door to the Present. This starts by acknowledging what activity I am engaged in and becoming clear that, given my options, I have chosen it. Next, I must commit to doing what I am doing and not casually condone proceeding in conflict. This practice is at least one way to begin stilling my mind, calming my body, and returning to a peaceful, God-connected mindset.

246

Where does this thought come from?

Today I will ask myself two questions: "How do I feel in this situation," and "How do I *want* to feel?" At any given time, I am either throwing my emotional weight into the balance of fear and separation or I am adding to the world's measure of hope and kindness. This can't be seen, of course, but it can certainly be felt. My ego thoughts are usually quite obvious, but if not, I can ask myself what source do I *believe* this line of thought is coming from. Self-honesty plugs me into my intuition.

247

Harmlessness is proactive.

Because minds are connected, "It's no one else's business" is an inaccurate assessment. Being consistently harmless—as opposed to just talking about it—bolsters this urge within the mental atmosphere of our circle of friends, our family, and in the world. Even if this statement were true only in small measure, a little gain is better than none. Although I have at times taken huge strides, usually I walk down the road to misery in very small steps.

248

Attacking back, even if only mentally, duplicates the original mistake.

As people go through the day, they can't help but teach. For instance, as we shop in a grocery store, we encounter individuals teaching consideration, impatience, good humor, preoccupation, self-importance, forbearance, irritation, and so on. If our mind is still, reading other people's attitudes is no more difficult than reading the individual mindsets of pets at an animal shelter. So no matter how much I would like to believe that I am keeping it to myself, for me to be judgmental teaches my faith in the value of making judgments, as does being dejected, cynical, fearful, and so on. Mind matters. It's impossible to engage in a high-minded counterattack.

249

No one can be judgmental without wanting to be.

This is my mind. If I didn't want to feel this way, I wouldn't. In trying to let go of a grievance, the question I must ask is, "Why do I *want* to judge my partner (my child, my friend, this stranger, that politician)?" Otherwise, I fall into the trap of trying to justify my feelings by reviewing and bolstering the case I have against them. I always have the choice of not adding fuel to the fire. Being a physical victim or a victim of circumstances may not be a choice, but being a mental victim always is.

250

"The easy way out" is to be mentally honest.

If I don't take responsibility for my attitude, my ego will simply play out its preprogrammed agenda. This would seem to be "less trouble," but it isn't, because the ego's agenda always includes turmoil and struggle. Today I will notice how hard it is to be at odds with everything—to feel superior, to be jealous, to be a victim, to judge—in short, how hard it is to be mentally dishonest.

251

Do I suspect
that what I am about to say
will make this person unhappy?
Then the urge to say it
is from my ego.

I can change the nature of my contribution to the world
I see, but I can't keep from contributing. Acknowledging
the part I play in relationship difficulties is not "taking
on guilt." Feeling guilty is a form of withdrawal.
Whereas acknowledging that no matter how small it is,
I contribute to any disturbance in a relationship, is a
step toward joining. Trying to measure my part and
compare it to the part played by the other person com-
pounds the original mistake. All I need to know is that if
I feel disturbed, I am in some way feeding the disturbance.

252

There are no limits on the effects of happiness.

Who really knows the effect of one happy thought? Certainly its impact on my immediate relationships is palpable. But is it also possible that it circles the globe, finding entry into any open heart, encouraging and giving hope in some unseen way? I am convinced it does. For whenever I am truly happy, I feel the warmth and presence of the like-minded, a growing family whose strength lies in their gentleness and whose message is in their treatment of others.

253

It's impossible to
feel our connection with others
and not be happy.

Happiness is inclusive. It's a myth that we can be
happy by "besting" another person. Favorable
circumstances and individual victories can be
elating, but there is no peace. A guilty sorrow that
we couldn't bring everyone with us seeps through
the splintered hull of euphoria. Whereas love is
a universal tide that lifts all ships equally.

254

It is good and right to be happy.
It is also the only way
I can be consistently kind to myself.

The psychology of our day emphasizes "empowering" the ego, protecting it with "boundaries," and actively betraying others through "honest communication." It makes the crucial mistake of assuming that it's possible to "first be kind to yourself," in other words, to start giving to our self while "temporarily" withholding from others. This would be possible only if we were not deeply connected, so deeply in fact that most sacred scriptures say we are one. Happiness is expansive and any persistent thought that we are not treating someone else as an equal undercuts its nature and reverses the experience.

255

I am free of the nature of the world, until I try to control it.

Is it possible to say, "Nothing will go right today?" and still be happy? It is, in fact, the essential first step. Because nothing will go right. Something will spill; certain people will be late; a thing needed will be lost, and then there's the neighbor's dog. Is there really any hope of eliminating forever all annoying smells, noises, poor workmanship, overpriced products, traffic snarls, and rudeness in stores? Not to mention disease, violence, and natural disaster. We have little chance of being happy if we pit ourselves against the basic nature of the world.

256

When the mind becomes
as still as the divine,
it becomes as happy as the divine.

As the song says, "You can't roller skate in a buffalo
herd, but you can be happy if you've a mind to."
The key is having a mind to. Those who are determined to be happy cannot fail, because the divine,
which surrounds and sustains us, is a great brilliance
and an endless joy.

257

Peace rests on a foundation
of understanding,
and happiness is sheltered
by a roof of tolerance.

Without the experience of connection with the
people, the creatures, and other living things around
us, we are left with the resources of a fragile body
and a brain-dependent mind. As this separated self
suffers the loss that time brings to all things, the
tragedy of living without love should become
increasingly apparent; yet our fear of equality blinds
us to the obvious. The way back to sanity is usually
traveled in baby steps, the first of which is our decision to be tolerant and understanding of at least one
other living thing. From that commitment, the stir-
rings of an ancient peace are felt rising in the soul.

258

In every kind heart
is a place of bliss.

There is a mental state that passes easily over the
endless nonsense that deranges the day. Like a
gentle breeze, it refreshes everything but disturbs
nothing. It is happy just being itself. Having
wholeness, it has wholeness to give.

259

Despite the world's shrill objection,
simply being good is enough.

If I hold to the impossible ideal that a world of
separate agendas can be perfected, my spiritual
efforts are thwarted and my emotions deteriorate
into cynicism. Hope in a better world is misplaced.
But the hope that I can be a better person within
the world is simply a matter of willingness.

260

How do I *want* to respond to what just happened?

The opposite of inner happiness is the state of mind that is constantly getting entangled and pulled down by almost everything that occurs. Containing no quiet core, it is vulnerable to confusion, fear, and loneliness. Each day presents a new and pointless obstacle course. Is this how I want to live? If it isn't, then let me remember these four magic words, "Don't take the bait."

261

When the heart's preference is heard, there is no fear.

The heart always answers for the present and in the present. It will guide you from where you are and speak directly to what you are doing. The heart's preference never fills the mind with empty longings or pointless fears. Its voice is filled with stillness.

262

There isn't anyone
who can't be treated kindly,
because how I treat others
is up to me, not up to them.

If tomorrow I find myself near death, how will I
wish I had been today? Will I wish I had relaxed a
little and enjoyed what could have been enjoyed?
Will I wish I had been more understanding of my
child, my partner, my friend? Will I wish I had
paused in stillness and felt the breath of God?

263

Today I will not disregard
my intuition of what this person
wants from me.

The mind can be trained, yet in most instances my thoughts are so chaotic and vulnerable to events that I go through the day looking at everyone through a swirling fog of ambiguity. This blocks my intuition of what each person is at heart. Yet it is seeing the deep and often unspoken urges of the heart that allows me to connect and that makes me happy.

264

Life is lived in the pauses,
not in the events.

Impatience wastes happiness. Sitting quietly in the
hush of dawn, I hear the waking sounds of earth
and see the shifts in light and shadow that my more
hurried mind would miss. Action without stillness
merely adds to the chaos of my life.

265

The joy within us is very still.
It is not physically slow;
it is simply at peace.

It's not uncommon to see a loving parent, grandparent, or even a teacher or child-care provider smiling and obviously at peace as little kids scream and run wildly around. Happiness doesn't require an accompanying picture. It requires connection.

266

Prejudging any situation blocks the possibility of being present.

Shakespeare writes, "There is nothing either good or bad, but thinking makes it so." What a relief! Because as it turns out, we have virtually no control over outcomes, yet we have complete control over our thoughts. Yet as I go through the day, I am amazed at how many conditions and activities I have pegged as good or bad. Hair, good; baldness, bad. House cleaning bad; having my chores done, good. Being the family member who gets the flu, bad; being the one who doesn't, good. Driving around looking for a parking space, bad; finding one quickly, good. No wonder I have such difficulty sensing God in the situation.

267

What meaning do I wish to give this event, those words, that person?

Our thoughts coat the world. The world has surprisingly little effect on our happiness until it is coated with our thoughts and thereby assigned its meaning for us. Today I will distinguish between what I am seeing and the significance I am giving it.

268

Looking at my day dispassionately is an act of love.

Disapproval begins in the mind and spreads throughout. It can't be confined to thoughts about just one event or person. When I disapprove, I cloak my world in pain. Furthermore, I have the false sense of being set apart from what I am seeing. And when I single out certain people as good—meaning "superior"—I now am in the first stage of the same loveless mistake.

269

When the focus
of my thoughts shifts
from separation to connection,
my entire world shifts with it.

The thoughts that I take to heart become the
eyes with which I see. Even if unconsciously, they
determine what I choose to overlook as insignifi-
cant. Yet simply because something goes unheeded
doesn't mean that I remain unaffected by it. This
is why being aware of my thoughts is crucial to
sustaining peace.

270

Is this thought a source of pain or a source of comfort?

Some things are more difficult to let go of than others. The trick is to commit to the process. I do the best I can each time I get caught up in attack thoughts, and I set no time limit on my future efforts. It will take as long as it takes, and I resolve not to stop until I can think of the event or the individual in peace.

271

All thoughts are circular.

However much I want to stand apart from my judgments, they remain an irritant to my mind, and any irritant, no matter how slight, is a complete block to inner comfort. This type of unhappiness is directionless, agitated, and above all arrogant. Since I think whatever I want to think, let me examine my motives honestly so that I can choose again.

272

Let me be done with guilt.
There is a song to sing.
There is life to live
and people to enjoy.

The irony of either assigning guilt or taking it on
myself is that whomever I make wrong, I will not
thereby perceive what is right in the other person.
Being certain of the power of darkness—which is
required in order to judge—does not increase my
perception of light.

273

Nothing has to "turn out well"
for me to be happy.
People don't have to
"behave themselves"
for me to love them. I am free.

When I release or "give up" the world, I am not left
with less, because there is another world waiting,
a spiritual counterpart that answers this dream of
disaster. God has recreated in beauty everything
I now see. Giving up the old world for the new can
only be done moment by moment. And it is never
done person by person. To have no attachments
doesn't mean to have no love. Love alone shows
me the new world.

274

All I need do
is make the effort.

I tend to forget how long and hard I have worked at being unhappy and how painstakingly I have learned the rules of misery. Am I now going to resent the little effort needed to *let go* of suffering?

275

Simply start over.

I want to know in advance every detail of my future course. Whether considering a new job, new friendship, new computer program, or simply ordering something new from the menu, I think I am due an exact accounting of the results before I begin. Since this is impossible, I never start. This is especially detrimental when I make a spiritual mistake and get bogged down over what went wrong instead of simply beginning again. To start over I must be willing to take myself as I am, to work with what I have, and to do so in the present. Mistakes need only be corrected.

276

Pause often in stillness.

To have peace, give peace. To be happy, make happy. To feel loved, love. This is very simple and is a part of all the world's inspired teachings. But it cannot be understood by a mind that refuses to pause.

277

There is a place in me that is already Home.

A busy mind is fear dominated, and trying to sit on my mind to make it be still is to be afraid of mind itself, which is a gift from God. Let me forget controlling my mind and remember opening my heart, for an open heart already includes the thoughts I share with God.

278

Don't be afraid to look at fear.

Anxiety has no practical value. It is a mind-clouding and soul-shrouding activity. It doesn't protect me against making mistakes. In fact, it hurts my perspective, scatters my concentration, and makes me more prone to error. However, this doesn't mean that anxiety should be resisted. It needs to be gently seen and calmly examined. "What is the thought behind this fear? And what is the thought behind that thought?"

279

Spiritual efforts often seem
phony and irrelevant.
Today I will pass through
this resistance and do
what will be helpful.

The object is to become more of what I am at my core, to become more real. Either I decide life or it decides me. Within one choice is strength, and hope based on vision, and an ever-expanding wholeness. Within its alternative is a spreading sense of powerlessness and unreality.

280

What I want is what I get.
To be conflicted is to want
the usual chaos.

My life reflects the unity or the division of my will.
A conflicted will means that I am in neutral and will
be pushed along by outside influences. Yet when I
take the time to see clearly what I want, and act on
it, I add direction to my life; in other words, I add
my self.

281

Letting the day dictate my mood is a decision.

Emotions are not my inner self. Nor are they
an irresistible force. If I calmly watch what I am
feeling, the emotion changes within minutes, if not
seconds. Additionally, there are layers of feeling at
any given instant. Emotions do not describe a single
self. The ego is as fractured and volatile as the
guidance it gives.

282

I will listen to my peace,
not to my ever-changing
ego emotions.

If I continue responding to the world in the old conflicted ways, I remain its victim, and my feelings of defeat and sorrow deepen with age. In just a little over a hundred years, the seven billion people now on this planet will all be dead. More will come to take their place, but their fate will be the same. My commitment to the world is therefore to a dream of quick and certain destruction. There is a way out, but am I willing to do what needs to be done? Am I willing to listen to and obey the part of my mind that is already awake?

283

I alone choose to look at
what "has my attention,"
and to look away
from everything else.

The ability to decide is merely the ability to give
attention. Whether or not I acknowledge it at the
time, I compile the evidence that makes my decision
logical. The happier approach to life is to notice
where the simplicity lies and to walk in that direction.

284

What I anticipate rarely happens.
How I choose to respond
to the present always happens.

If I try to decide against certain circumstances
occurring in my life, I lose. But when I peacefully
and kindly plan how to bypass their usual impact
on my emotions, I win.

285

Today I will nurture happiness.

At first, our moments of happiness are like the tiny
green shoots of a new plant. They are fragile and
vulnerable to disruption. Unless we give them room
to grow, they wither away, and this has already
happened too many times in my life. Today I will
be alert to any seed of happiness, and I will clear a
space for it to grow. I will water it with my attention
and nourish it with my commitment.

286

Deciding to be happy doesn't change external circumstances, but it will appear to.

Would you incessantly skirmish over how things should go and people should be if you knew that a great field of peace surrounds these tiny places of war and that all you have to do to enter it is decide that you would rather be happy? By consciously choosing to be happy, you leave the battlefield.

287

There is no spiritual necessity
to master any given aspect
of the world.

Often the simplest way to rid our life of what seems
to be a chronic problem is not to "tackle it head
on" but to find a way around it. Since problems
never reoccur in exactly the same form, it's usually
incorrect that we have to "learn to deal with it."
It may sometimes be simpler to confront a given
situation directly, but an indirect approach often
makes the world less sticky. For instance, avoiding
certain people, places, or circumstances is not
always a mistake. Today I will look for ways to live
more simply.

288

Today I will avoid being self-willed.
I will set no goals that are
not shared with the divine.

Many people look back and see that their parents'
advice to "see it through" was unnecessary and
unhelpful. Doggedly persisting "to the bitter end" is
not necessarily courageous or wise. Being willful is
closed-minded. It should be obvious that it's happier
to walk freely rather than with bloodied feet.

289

Happiness is flexible.

Why does everything have to be finished? Why does every "realistic" movie have to be watched to its depressing conclusion, every party attended until someone else leaves first, every argument pursued until the last bitter exchange, every stab of sadness or depression endlessly analyzed, every grievance milked dry? The only thing I have to carry through on is kindness—to others and to myself.

290

I will never know peace as long as I condone attack thoughts.

My ego mind can manufacture euphoria, excitement, hubris, passivity, lethargy, and a kind of short-lived satisfaction or "closure." But I can't of myself create peace. Peace is of God and God is love. I will know I am serious about experiencing the peace of God when I consistently and instantly challenge any unloving thought, no matter how fleeting.

291

If I choose the present,
within that instant
I cannot choose the past.

It's often said that we can forgive but we can't
forget. Yet to forgive in a way that restores my mind
to wholeness, I must fail to keep recalling—and this
is decidedly not a hopeless objective. If I'm honest,
I must admit that I select from the past exactly what
I wish to give power to.

292

Today I will remember the Self I share with others and with my Source.

One of the reasons I chew on what was done to me is that I gain a sense of moral superiority by comparing my role to the role played by the other person. But look at the price I pay for this concocted sense of virtue. I must embrace a damaged sense of self, then I must be vigilant to feel and act like a person who has been wronged. Today I have no use for satisfaction derived from comparisons.

293

When my mind focuses on a failure, it's imbued with the sadness of the subject. When it focuses on Truth, it heals and grows strong.

I must acknowledge all weaknesses and shortcomings if I am serious about healing my attitudes and strengthening my motivation. However, that is not my intent if all I do is stay sprawled in a pool of old sins and chronic inadequacies. The ego justifies cruel thoughts and destructive behavior by first telling itself that *it* is the injured party. Failure can be either a reason to attack or a reason to improve. Only one of those choices makes my life a positive factor in the world.

294

Today I will look at how far
I have come rather than
how far I still have to go.

It's not making a mistake, but remaining within that
past event, that shatters my mind. Self-censure is
neither virtuous, humble, nor honest.

295

When I wallow in a mistake,
I merely get more of it all over me.

One of the most perverse hindrances to peace and
mental wholeness is eliminated when we learn to
react to a mistake—no matter its flagrancy or
persistence—by simply acknowledging it and
beginning again. Today I will remember that
redemption is always possible, but that past
wrongs can only be made right in the present.

296

There are many ways to a peaceful mind.

Difficult situations are made more difficult by ruling out the small steps that could help. Today I will neutralize my desire for complexity by acknowledging the obvious. I'll not hesitate to look straight at what usually happens that upsets me. Whatever the difficulty, there is a way past it—that is, there is a way for me to have peace. Actually, there are many ways, and I will see at least a few of them if I will set aside my self-imposed restrictions, take time to look at what is going on, and not be too picky about which means I use to put the problem behind me.

297

Deciding how an event should go does not control the event.

From the moment they get out of bed, most people begin unconsciously practicing the mistake of deciding in advance how each little event should go—how long it should take, how they should perform, how circumstances should unfold. And as usual, the day perversely refuses to go along. The great common gate through which most annoyances and irritations attack my peace is expectation. This despite the fact that no one can predict precisely what they will be doing even five minutes from now. When I buy into my ego's expectations, I immediately forsake my present mental stability.

298

I can chase the future,
but only the present
can be caught.

A surprising amount of my frustration is over what
I can't possibly do anything about. It has already
happened, or it's something that will never happen,
or it may happen in some general way but there is
nothing I can do about it now. Since I can always
be helpful to myself or others this instant, when
I notice my mind trying to solve the impossible,
I will stop and ask myself if an unattainable pursuit
is more desirable than the potentials of the present.

299

Row gently down the stream.

As we row our boat "gently down the stream,"
we let the shore come to us. We don't command,
implore, or try to "visualize" the shore into looking
a certain way around the next bend in the river.
It will be what it will be. And so we relax and enjoy
the ride. In precisely the same manner, I can let
the day come to me and greet each unfolding event
with tolerance and ease—and whenever possible,
with amusement.

300

I will not disregard the symbolism of my behavior.

Mental peace is not necessarily protected by behavior that appears peaceful. On occasion, it might be more conducive to spiritual progress to file a complaint, join a picket line, demand better service, play a body-contact sport, or enlist in the armed forces. But usually these are not the kinds of daily choices before us. In most encounters, behavior that symbolizes kindness promotes mental wholeness and connection more than behavior that appears aggressive, controlling, adversarial, or selfish.

301

Truthfulness is within the heart, not within mere words.

Courtesy, cordiality, and politeness usually serve my peace of mind because my actions are less likely to stir up the individuals around me. Appearances, in and of themselves, have no depth, and certainly manners and protocol are mere appearances. Yet it doesn't follow that an in-your-face approach is more sincere or truthful. Some appearances facilitate a simple life better than others. An important part of awareness is being conscious of the probable effect that my words and actions will have on others, as well as on my own mind.

302

To be comfortable with other people's lack of understanding, I must first acknowledge my own.

It has been well said that, "To understand all is to forgive all." However, this doesn't mean that the most effective approach to forgiveness is to strive for perfect understanding. No matter how much I increase it, I still will not understand "all." This fact alone should motivate me to acknowledge an understanding greater than my own, one so complete that it has no need to forgive.

303

The perfect outcome can be sought
only in the future—
where it is destined to remain.

Whenever I find myself looking to the future to be
complete, I will remember that God doesn't ask me
to make myself worthy. If I knew how to prepare
myself to receive God, my knowledge would already
be perfect. It is in recognizing that I don't really
know anything for sure that I open my mind to
the divine.

304

My ego focuses on
eventual improvement.
My deeper self focuses on
my present state of mind.

Fear is the belief that the future may in some way
duplicate the past. There is usually very little to fear
within the moment. My dread of making a mistake
rests on the conviction that what has happened to
me in the past is more important than my present
mental state. But nothing is more important than
my present mental state.

305

Forgiveness is vision free of the past.

A judgmental feeling about another person is based on the same belief as my fear of making mistakes: I think that what someone once did is more important than how the person is now. The work before me is to practice fully absorbing people as they are this instant. Taking them in as if for the first time. Obviously, I won't accomplish this if their past dominates my perception.

306

Simply forgive
and be happy.

Forgive, but do not wonder how you must act.
Forgive, but do not try to convince another to
forgive. Forgive, but do not hold yourself superior
that you have done so. Simply forgive. Wrap your
forgiveness around you like a cloak of light, a
spiritual barrier that protects your happiness and
your peace, but closes no one out.

307

Laughter unites.

The ego's version of laughter engenders feelings of separation. It always makes people uneasy on some level. But true laughter is the most beautiful sound on earth. As it rings in one heart, it resonates in all others. It is a shower of enjoyment that falls on all things equally and refreshes each one.

308

As the ego shrinks,
joy expands.

Once, when we were quite small, we somehow knew not to let things become so real. The world danced before us because we looked at it through dancing eyes. This is still possible, but for it to happen I must become small again.

309

I have a past,
but only I can bring it
into the present.

A sure way to stay unhappy is to be protective of
the past that I have so painstakingly accumulated.
My body is a symbol. It is the past seen within
the moment. And I insist that others take it into
consideration because I believe it is my identity.
But a body can also reflect a divine presence. One
reason most little children are so happy and have
such boundless energy is that they have very little
past to drag behind them. This allows their minds
to function as designed. Basically, they process only
the present, which is the dwelling place of God.

310

Be as willing to be happy as a little child.

In the realm of the world, we are our children's teachers, but in the realm of the divine, they are here to teach and guide us. Today, whenever I remember, I will release my adult rigidity and be a kid again.

311

Wear not your spiritual beliefs like jewelry. Cherish them secretly within your heart.

We come into the world unencumbered by "formative experience" and free of anxiety about the implications of what has already occurred. Our first experience of this is a gift; our second experience must be learned, practiced, and protected. If we use our episodes of light and our insights of oneness to exhibit how special we are, we sabotage our progress and must begin again. The effort needed can and should be pleasant. But only sustained effort leads to sustained peace.

312

When our gaze is on the present
and our eyes laugh,
we shine on the world we see
and the light of our heart
goes before us.

The experience of a world filled with light is possible
because light is already within us. We are something
more than a body, and once this something becomes
more interesting to us than our life's residue of
fear and failure, we begin to notice that the reality
within us is also within the images we behold.

313

A fear-free mind heals
because it gives hope.
Without a word spoken or withheld,
it encourages and calms.

Healing is a natural consequence of the fact that all
minds are joined. This is why it's never necessary
for me to "keep someone from making a mistake,"
"show them the light," or instruct them on how to
behave. When I practice peace, it is the same peace
that already rests in every heart. When I strengthen
my own faith, this bolsters the faith that others
have in what is already theirs, and they in turn
strengthen me.

314

If I know how to make an individual angry, I certainly know them well enough to make them happy.

Today I will trust my own sense of happiness, of what makes me happy and what does not. I will allow this sense to encompass my diet, my appearance, my relationships, my body, and my choice of activities. I will let it spread to my spending and my saving, to my health and my habitat. And in so far as I can, I will also extend it to those around me.

315

Be single-minded.

Be purposeful. Be focused. Know who you are and what you truly want. Be conscious. Be aware. Formulate your purpose into words. Etch it on your heart. Repeat it in your mind. And gently live it as this day unfolds.

316

The answer is quietly heard and quietly held.

Let the roots of your knowing deepen and expand. Water them with your patience and your clear purpose. Where is the shame in admitting that you have not yet arrived? Let the world rant about who is right, then respectfully return your heart to the quiet answer.

3I7

To know truth,
practice truth.

Simply practice knowing and you will know.
Practice trusting and you will have the grounds
for trust. Practice your heart and you will be happy.
Practice your self and you will know a self that
touches all things in peace.

318

My anxiety always indicates a conflicted purpose.

When my heart has only one voice, I am free.
As I work to know myself and become one thing,
I stop fearing my own will because I stop doubting
my own goodness. In this way I see why goodness
is not confined to me.

3I9

Today I will see no one unlike myself.

I am vigilant to note every little mistake made by my family, friends, and everyone else who crosses my mind. Yet if I wish to see the perfection in others, I must first acknowledge the imperfections in myself. It should be clear that I will never know oneness until I experience equality with those around me. Face it, we're all pretty screwed up, and it's just plain silly to value one form of insanity over another. Nothing justifies believing that I know more or am further along than someone else, because inequality is spiritually impossible.

320

I seek your peace.

If I am unhappy, I can restore my happiness by silently saying to whomever is before me: "I seek your peace. What am I not giving you? What can I give you now?" But if I am happy and want to be unhappy, I can think instead: "I seek my personal pleasure. What am I not getting from you? What do I need from you now?"

321

Happiness
is our job.

As the workday nears, and as it begins to unfold, watch it gently and without suspicion. Take each task as it comes, and don't peer over it to the next task. Do that task impeccably, but don't expect acknowledgment. In fact, expect nothing at all from the job or from anyone in the workplace. Approached in this way, work can be happy, because happiness remains within our control.

322

Held in stillness,
any form of fear will dissolve.

No matter what the form or degree, if fear is taken to heart, it blocks the experience of peace. Anxiety, dread, depression, worry, and all other forms of fear are offerings from my ego that do not have the power to "grab" my attention. They don't arise from reason or from truth. I am free to quietly observe any kind of fear, and if I will simply look at it, inner stillness can guide my actions. But the moment I assume that any solitary passing emotion is "the way I feel," I lose control of my mind.

323

Destiny can only be seen in peace.

Our pathway through life is seen in retrospect. There is a sense in which everything does add up, but not in advance of the steps taken. If our journey is guided by the present instead of by a hodgepodge of fears about the future, we begin to discern a lovely wake flowing behind our actions, including even our mistakes. There is a beauty, a just-rightness, within the course of our life, but worry and second-guessing blind us to it.

324

Only decisions made in peace
can be carried out in peace.

There is no right thought about any issue or
difficulty, yet the ego searches ceaselessly to come
up with one. Ultimately, this mental agitation is
more distressing than the problem I face. There are
countless good ways to proceed but only one good
motivation. Any time I act in peace, I ensure peace
of mind within the outcome.

325

**All that is right,
all that is meaningful,
resides in God.**

It's not possible to think correctly about what is not God. However, it is possible to allow God to do the thinking. When something upsetting occurs, gently refuse to cast about for the best or "highest" position to take. Instead, turn to God and say, "Show me how you look at this," and God will give you an experience rather than an opinion.

326

Anger is never justified.

The simple acknowledgment that God does not judge the person I am judging begins to undercut my certainty that my anger is justified.

327

Forgiveness
is never dishonest.

Forgiveness is not some futile exercise in rosy self-deception. It's never a positive reinterpretation of events that I lay on top of the negative interpretation I already believe. It's simply the gift I give to myself that allows me to return to the present and be as God created me.

328

There is no anger at our core,
which is joined with God.

Because anger never occurs on the deepest level, it
can be relinquished without hypocrisy. To see what
I truly want clears my mind of superficial passions,
and even of chronic bitterness.

329

Do I want the identity formed by my past or the identity created by God?

Most of us have abundant reason to be angry and feel wounded about things that have been done to us. But eventually we ask ourselves if—despite the justification—we wish to remain the picture of damage that we believe another person caused. The part of us that is joined with God is untouched by human history, but when the mind dwells on the past, that part of us is made inaccessible.

330

Blessings are never comparative.

The lesson that all criticism attacks the criticizer is difficult to learn. It appears to undercut the way humans maintain their sense of self-worth—which is that one is thought more highly of when one sees to it that someone else is thought less highly of. This is called succeeding or winning, yet it defeats the soul. The only true blessings we can receive have been given to all. Otherwise, we hold them for a moment only, even as we watch them slip through our hands.

331

The goal of happiness and the means of happiness must be congruent.

It's *possible* to be "open and honest" with individuals without attacking them—but that's seldom how honesty and openness are practiced. If "honoring our feelings" is the goal, it's also possible to beat pillows, scream into the wind, go for a walk, meditate, describe the sensations to ourselves in detail, or release our bodily tensions in some other harmless way. It's curious that we think that in order to be true to our self, we must hurt someone else. Pain, including our own, never promotes peace.

332

The longer I judge,
the more I become
like the person I am judging.

The rule for restoring peace of mind is: *Do not allow criticism to leave your mind. Do not project it or act it out. Remove its source, then repair the damage to your mind quickly.* Even though the source of criticism is the desire to criticize, this rule entails no actual sacrifice. To the contrary, the longer I dwell on another's weakness, the weaker I become.

333

When a judgmental
line of thought ends,
the damage it caused the mind
ends with it.

The world may not be fair, but Love is. All things
done in and with Love are accompanied by a whole
and healed mind.

334

To look so carefully at our anger
that we see through it to our heart
is to use the mind's
most powerful corrective force.

In a world of projections and meanings based on
the past, vision is omnipotent. First vision brings
correction. Then it brings the Reality that waits
beyond correction. If at any time it isn't obvious
what I should do spiritually, I can always increase
stillness, because stillness cannot project, and being
an activity of present-mindedness, it will never
interpret from the past.

335

The kingdom of heaven is within.

To say there is a Plan, that everything fits, that there is meaning to it all, is an absurd if not outrageous concept in light of the cruelty and unfairness of the world. And the horrors of "Mother Nature" are no less numerous or extreme than the horrors of humanity. Yet now and again the clouds of perception part, and for just a moment we know that all is well, that we are all watched over by One who knows and loves us, and that in a way that makes no sense to the body's eyes and the body's brain, everything that happens is anticipated and blessed.

336

God's creation is one.
Nothing can divide it.

We walk together, as do all those who have ever laid strife aside and set their eyes on love. This is "the other way" to pass through the world. It requires no profound concepts, no excluding vocabulary, no correct beliefs, only enough hope in the possibility of love and peace to pursue them in our family, on the streets, in the stores, on the job.

337

Simply keep a place in you
where it is welcome, and peace
will come and abide with you.

If God's work is complete, so must be the work of
God's children. I can deny this fact or I can embrace
it. But if I deny it, the only power I have is to
deceive myself, because the oneness of Truth cannot
be undone. Eternity is pure blessing, unchanging
and whole; my job is merely to accept the gift.

338

To let go is simply to rest from sacrifice.

The root meaning of the verb "to forgive" is "to let go, to give back, to cease to harbor." Looked at this way, forgiveness is a restful activity. Far more work is required to cling to a judgment than to let go of it. What is relinquished is not valuable, and what at first may seem like a sacrifice is soon experienced as a gift.

339

Those who don't forgive
have not yet begun to live.

The only way we become convinced of the benefits
of forgiveness is to start forgiving. Teaching or
studying forgiveness without actually doing it is
like studying or teaching breathing without taking a
breath. Life shifts so dramatically once forgiveness
becomes habitual that one's old life is looked back
on as empty and meaningless.

340

In trying to convince someone
of the truth of Oneness,
I only demonstrate
my belief in division.

The great neglected need in this era of rigid,
clashing opinions is the need for direct experience.
Once we experience a spiritual fact, we stop arguing
about it or trying to convince others that we are
right. As long as we feel a need to influence another
person's opinions about Truth, it remains for us a
concept, something that perhaps we accept intellec-
tually, but not a thing that fills our perceptions with
light and our heart with equality.

341

Where does the light of God end and I begin?

Divine light doesn't travel just so far and stop.
We were created by Light, in Light, and of Light.
We can believe in darkness, anticipate darkness,
and be preoccupied with past thoughts and present
perceptions of darkness, but we cannot change our
basic nature. We can't recreate what the divine has
already created. When we feel happy and connected,
we are beginning to experience ourselves as we are.

342

Heaven on earth is up to me.

A decision must be made, and it can be made now. It is simply this: "I will begin." And what must we begin? We must try to be kind now—not appear kind, but be kind. We must make the effort, no, the struggle, to be happy now—and not first gain what we "need" in order to be happy. We can't just add the concepts of kindness and happiness to our life. They must be our life.

343

I always get what I want,
provided I want it
without conflict.

It's impossible to want something for myself alone
and not be conflicted, because those I am connected
to are left out. If I am conflicted, it takes an endless
effort to walk past my ordinary way of doing things.
Yet time and again I have seen that once I have decided
to make that effort, and have committed myself
completely, all of it becomes surprisingly easy.

344

Annoyance and impatience are indicative of a loveless mindset that requires immediate correction.

My goal to be happy and kind and at peace will allow for no secondary aim. I can't hope to bring my life to peace and also take time out to be irritated. Irritation won't add to my chances for happiness.

345

Peace, not perfection, is my goal.

Naturally, we make mistakes. In fact, all we do is make mistakes. If we stopped making mistakes, we would ascend. So, becoming perfect is not a reasonable goal, but losing my fear of mistakes is. The correct response to a mistake is to look at it, acknowledge that I made it, ask myself what I can do differently next time, then quickly start over and return to peace.

346

Honest and specific acknowledgment
of my own fallibility
allows connection with others
to come more easily.

If I think I am more spiritual, wiser, or further
along than other people, any mistake I make will
be jolting. But "trials" are an opportunity to make
a better choice this time around. And mistakes
indicate the realities of my present state of progress
and thus are an invitation to move another step
forward in a specific direction. My struggles soften
as I realize that we all struggle together.

347

God calls us
to consider our freedom,
not our guilt.

Don't spend one instant chewing on a mistake.
To do so releases poison into the psyche. Simply
choose a path different from the faulty one already
tried. And as you walk, your head held high, notice
the smile of welcome toward which you move.

348

Never think of a mistake you made
without remembering the loving
presence of the One who was there
at the time and did not judge you.

Picturing the divine within the past is closer to the
Truth than picturing a scene devoid of Light. I can't
change the past, but I can transform it. God was
there when it happened, embracing me and everyone.
By adding this Truth to the memory, I heal the
source of pain.

349

Awareness, not guilt,
is the healing response
to painful patterns.

Properly seen, behavioral patterns are artifacts in
the museum of life. They are little chunks of our
history that invite exploration. Ask yourself, "How
does this pattern work? What does it usually attach
itself to? How does it come? How does it go? And
why does it stay?" This is not dwelling on a mistake,
but unraveling it to make it powerless.

350

If my goal is peace, then meeting my ego needs must serve that purpose.

Our ego needs must be met or handled in some way or else they build up and become increasingly urgent. But there is a difference between the actual need and our usual way of meeting it. Today I will not run from the first signs that a need is surfacing. I will stop and examine it calmly. Then I will open my mind fully and allow myself to think of alternative ways of meeting it.

351

Look for your willingness
and you will find it.
Wait on your strength
and it will build.

I may be aware of a mistake at the time I am making
it, try halfheartedly to check myself, then "willfully"
continue being wrong. None of that matters spiritually if, as soon as I see that I am strong enough to
do so, I start over in some modest way. Eventually
I must learn not to indulge destructive desires in any
form, but until I reach that point, the appropriate
response to a mistake is to ask myself, "How might
I begin to correct it?"

352

Progress is measured
in the number of times we try,
not the number of times we fail.

Starting over has a cumulative effect because we show our mind that our love of goodness is greater than our love of suffering. It isn't necessary to first have faith in ourselves. When you think about it, this is an impossible goal when attempting something we have never tried. But trying in itself calls on a deeper reserve, where faith has been replaced with certainty.

353

Organization and planning are more spiritual than nonchalance and chaos.

There's a tendency to assume that spiritual beliefs should be acted on in uncommon ways. For example, as a sign of faith, to spend money we don't have. Or to act as if we are "unconcerned with appearances." But living contrary to the norms proves nothing. The world tends to be less preoccupying if we fit in rather than stand apart. If taking a strong moral stand is required, then of course, we do so. But, in general, those who work, dress, interact with family members, and carry on conversations in a natural way invite fewer problems because they are less likely to agitate other people's attitudes.

354

God cares about me,
about everyone, about everything.
To do all things with care
is to do all things with God.

The inner qualities we bring to our daily activities,
and not the form they take, determine the degree
of connection and peace we experience. One career
is no less spiritual than another, one household task
no less holy, and one friend or companion no less
a child of God.

355

When I approach
any task indifferently,
I abandon God
and I abandon who I am.

To anticipate greater happiness in an upcoming
activity than the one I am engaged in is to overlook
where the divine is located. When I do what is
before me impeccably, kindly, and peacefully, I do
it in the company of angels.

356

Do all things
as if for your Beloved.

Once God's love is felt, all problems of motivation
cease. And yet, when I feel no divine connection,
I can still live my life as if the connection were still
there, because in Truth it is. No block to peace can
long endure an open heart and a willing mind.
Today I will dedicate each meal, each task, each
activity to God.

357

Within Love, nothing is lost
and no one is far away.

What is God but a home full of welcome? What is God but a life free of fear? What is God but a presence that comforts and makes us forever safe? What is God but the answer to every question we have ever asked?

358

The past is God with me.
The present is God with me.
The future is God with me.
It's always the same time.

In God there is no time because nothing is out of reach and no change is needed. Time is a dungeon of our own construction. If time were a reality equal to God, it could not be said that time flies, yet also drags, that it can be saved as well as lost, that it can be on our hands, yet out of our hands, and that we can possess it while still longing for time out or time off. Not once does time cradle the infant of peace in its arms and smile into the innocent eyes of the blessed present.

 **359**

The loveless sounds of the world recede before the song of God.

The world sings because we make of it a song. It dances because we take its hand and lead it in dance. We were given dominion over the earth when we were given dominion over our heart.

360

Walk in gentleness.

What the ego made, the mind can undo. Only
the single purpose of harmlessness is required.
A harmless mind extends in all directions and
throughout all time. Those who walk in gentleness
walk on holy ground.

361

All that is needed
is a leap in faith.

I freely give my faith to rumors, stories in the news,
and the latest nutritional supplement. Why not give
it to what I profess to believe? Why not think, act,
and feel as if I have a Friend, and that Friend is
here, and that Friend can be trusted—with my life,
my relationships, and my redemption?

362

Don't be afraid to gaze
into God's loving eyes and
know that you are cherished.

It's arrogant to think that God has pets and you
are the one singled out as unlovable. In true
humility, look into the still mirror of peace and see
your likeness.

363

What is there to feel
but the touch of peace?
What is there to see
but the face of God?
Where is there to go
but into the arms of Love?

Dear God, I don't know the way to you, but you know the way to me. I therefore resign as my own guide. There is no harm in waiting if I wait until I know your will. Let me not identify with any thought until I know your thoughts. Let me not decide where I am until I see your surrounding grace. Let me not say who I am until I know the Self you call your own.

364

May I offer God's gifts
in joy.

Gentle child of God, remind yourself of this truth:
You are a stream that has begun to flow in an old
and dry bed. You are a bringer of rain to earth that
is parched and dead. You are a breeze that renews
yet stops not to be thanked. From this time on you
may offer a cup of cool water to everyone you meet
or think about, to those yet to come, and to those
who have been here and left. There is no limit to
what you may give.

365

I stand in God.
I stand in Love.

Beloved of God, now you offer light to shine away the cold shadows of fear. You offer, but you do not manipulate or force. You merely stand within the Presence and feel the gratitude of God pour through you onto all those who receive God's gifts, and the blessing of God on all those not yet ready to receive. Resolve now to remain as constant in your giving as is your Source, and soon you will awake in the loving arms of the One you never left.

About the Author

Hugh Prather is the author of twenty books including the best-selling *Notes to Myself*, *How to Live in the World and Still Be Happy*, *The Little Book of Letting Go*, and *Standing on My Head*. He lives with Gayle, his wife and co-author of forty years, in Tucson, Arizona where for many years they were resident ministers at St. Francis in the Foothills United Methodist Church. Hugh is also the host of Everyday Wisdom with Hugh Prather on Wisdom Radio and Sirius Satellite Radio. Hugh and Gayle have three sons and a dog who thinks she's a cat.

To Our Readers

Conari Press, an imprint of Red Wheel/Weiser, publishes books on topics ranging from spirituality, personal growth, and relationships to women's issues, parenting, and social issues. Our mission is to publish quality books that will make a difference in people's lives—how we feel about ourselves and how we relate to one another. We value integrity, compassion, and receptivity, both in the books we publish and in the way we do business.

Our readers are our most important resource, and we value your input, suggestions, and ideas about what you would like to see published. Please feel free to contact us, to request our latest book catalog, or to be added to our mailing list.

Conari Press
An imprint of Red Wheel/Weiser, LLC
P.O. Box 612
York Beach, ME 03910-0612
www.conari.com